DEALING *with* MEETINGS YOU CAN'T STAND

Meet Less and Do More

Dr. Rick Brinkman

NEW YORK CHICAGO SAN FRANCISCO ATHENS
LONDON MADRID MEXICO CITY MILAN
NEW DELHI SINGAPORE SYDNEY TORONTO

1 2 3 4 5 6 7 8 9   QFR   22 21 20 19 18 17

ISBN 978-1-259-86307-3
MHID   1-259-86307-7

e-ISBN 978-1-259-86308-0
e-MHID   1-259-86308-5

Meeting Jet, Holographic Thinking, Conscious Communicator, and Conscious Communication University are trademarks of Rick Brinkman Productions, Inc. Conscious Communication is the registered trademark of Rick Brinkman Productions, Inc.

Illustrations by Geraldine Charette

Book design by Lee Fukui and Mauna Eichner

Library of Congress Cataloging-in-Publication Data

Names: Brinkman, Rick, author.
Title: Dealing with meetings you can't stand: meet less and do more / Dr. Rick Brinkman.
Description: 1 Edition. | New York : McGraw-Hill Education, 2017.
  Identifiers: LCCN 2017001165 (print) | LCCN 2017014697 (ebook) | ISBN 9781259863080 () | ISBN 1259863085 () | ISBN 9781259863073 (paperback) | ISBN 1259863077
Subjects: LCSH: Business meetings. | Business communication. | Psychology, Industrial. | BISAC: BUSINESS & ECONOMICS / Business Communication / Meetings & Presentations.
Classification: LCC HF5734.5 (ebook) | LCC HF5734.5 .B75 2017 (print) | DDC 658.4/56--dc23
LC record available at https://lccn.loc.gov/2017001165

McGraw-Hill Education books are available at special quantity discounts to use as premiums and sales promotions or for use in corporate training programs. To contact a representative, visit the Contact Us pages at www.mhprofessional.com.

Each one of us makes a difference.

This is dedicated to you being an agent of change,

one who turns conflict and polarization

into communication and cooperation.

Contents

PART IV
IMPLEMENTING THE MEETING JET PROCESS

Acknowledgments

So many people contribute to our coming to each moment in time, I am overwhelmed with considering how to acknowledge them all.

Certainly my mother and father, who survived Auschwitz and came to New York City, where I was raised. With special thanks to my mother, who, when I was five years old and said, "I want to be a garbage collector," replied with, "When you finish medical school, you can be anything you want." Which led me to becoming a naturopathic doctor, an evidence-based physician focused on wellness, health restoration, and optimal health (see naturopathic.org).

Thanks to Dr. Doughton, who in my senior year shifted my focus to mind-body medicine and how communication and relationships affect our health and well-being.

To my good friend, naturopathic doctor colleague, and coauthor Dr. Rick Kirschner, with whom I took the journey of communication and seminars, armed with a costume trunk and a mission to change the world for the better.

To the American Association of Naturopathic Physicians for putting up with my seven-year reign of terror on the board, where much of this was incubated.

To Lisa, my wife of 38 years, for being the brilliant artist and thoughtful therapist that she is and for enabling an environment in our home of creativity that fosters the creation of works such as this.

To my daughter, Carle, for being so much fun as a kid—and as an adult, living her values and making a positive difference in the world.

And to my feline friends, Neelix and Leela, who sit patiently on my desk purring, waiting for me to take a break so we can go out for a walk together.

DEALING *with* MEETINGS YOU CAN'T STAND

PART I
THE PROBLEMS
with MEETINGS

The Problems with Meetings We Will Solve

*If you had to identify, in one word, the reason why
the human race has not achieved, and never will achieve,
its full potential, that word would be meetings.*

—DAVE BARRY

I remember the first business meeting I attended. Fresh out of naturopathic medical school, I was a new resident at the school clinic. We had a clinic conference meeting once a week with all the doctors. I thought the purpose was to be informed of anything we needed to know, discuss any issues we had, and, most of all, have an opportunity to ask the senior doctors questions about our cases. We sat in a circle in an uncomfortably small room. The clinic director began to talk. Nothing he was saying had anything to do with why I thought we were there. Then he free associated from one topic to another . . . I'm sure you get the picture. I counted the people in the room, since I thought we all were supposed to have a chance to speak, and I noticed the number of minutes left on the clock. It was simple math to see that there was no way that was going to happen. Then I tuned back in to the clinic director, who was droning on in a hypnotic monotone. That day I vowed, once I had my own practice, never to let myself get into meetings that I could not control.

Have you ever been in a meeting that was a complete waste of time? Or listened to someone go on and on, wondering, "What's the point?" Have you experienced conflicts at a meeting in which some people were trying to bully others to get their way? Or perhaps you have been with people who shoot down any idea. And then there are those who just don't participate. You never hear from them, and they don't contribute to decisions, but they are always happy to complain about those decisions later. Perhaps you've been at meetings that easily could have been accomplished in half the time. Maybe you've even experienced one in which you weren't sure why you were meeting at all.

I have good news and bad news. First the bad news: meetings are a necessity. But the good news is this: most people hate meetings. Therefore, even if you don't run the meetings, if you suggest to the person in charge, "Would you like to try a process that makes our meetings more focused, shorter, and more effective?" it's a rare human being who will respond with, "No, we wouldn't want that!"

According to a study by the Wharton Center for Applied Research, senior executives spend an average of 23 hours per week in meetings, and middle managers 11 hours. And according to senior and middle managers, 44 percent of these meetings are unproductive.[1]

Harvard Business Review found that 15 percent of an organization's total collective time is spent in meetings and that percentage has increased every year since 2008.[2]

A 2015 Harris Poll survey found that the number one obstacle to getting work done is having to attend **meetings**![3]

In the software provider Lucid Meetings' 2015 review of the literature on meetings, it was estimated that there were 36 to 56 million meetings held each day in the United States alone. It was estimated that the cost of unnecessary and unproductive meetings was between $70 and $283 billion a year![4]

Keep in mind that those figures do not factor in the value of the thousand other important things you should be doing but are not doing because you are in a meeting.

THE FOUR CATEGORIES OF PROBLEMS AT MEETINGS

I have been teaching communication for over 30 years, and in my research I have found the problems at meetings tend to consistently fall into four categories: preparation, people, process, and time. What follows are some of the greatest hits of issues, the Top 40, if you will, that I have heard over the years. See how many you've experienced and what others you're aware of that fall into these categories.

Preparation

- No clear agenda or purpose

- A poorly written agenda

- Starting with "Any other business," thereby opening up the agenda

- Personal agendas

- Items on the agenda that don't relate to everyone

- Regular meetings, whether or not they are necessary
- Not having the right people at the meeting
- Having too many people there

People

- People competing to speak
- People who dominate
- People who are unprepared
- People who don't say anything
- People who waffle
- People who are always negative
- People who go on and on to hear themselves talk
- People who don't listen to others
- People who are know-it-alls
- Personality clashes
- People not showing up

Process

- No clear process
- Catching people up who are late
- Unproductive debate over what can't be controlled
- Boring
- Mobile phones

- Stray comments

- Sarcastic comments, sniping

- Side conversations

- Multitasking

- Tangents

- No order to speak

- Not focused on priorities

- Not focused on action

Time

- People arriving late

- Not starting on time

- Insufficient time planned for topics, as well as the meeting

- Not ending on time

- Too long

- Poor timekeeping

- Meetings that overlap so that there is no journey time to the next meeting

- Too many meetings

Do any of these sound familiar? But like it or not, business needs to be conducted via meetings.

That is why I developed the Meeting Jet process. Think of people at meetings as passengers on a plane. They are trapped together in a contained space for a period of time. The flight or meeting may be delayed and may not start on time. The flight or meeting can go off course or even be hijacked. The flight or meeting may end late and cause the passengers or meeting participants to miss other connections or meetings. The flight or meeting can be uncomfortable or seem like a waste of time. And on contentious issues, people can bring too much baggage.

This is Dr. Rick, your pilot, speaking. I have good news. It doesn't take very long to transform a meeting because my method addresses all the problems of preparation, people, process, and time. I will show you how to apply the Meeting Jet process to all types of meetings, and it can be adapted depending on the number of people, the formality, and whether the meeting is virtual or face-to-face.

When people have a meeting process that works, meetings can actually be exciting and energizing events because people become part of something greater than themselves. The Meeting Jet process consistently accomplishes this. I'm going to make it easy for you. Over the last 20 years, I have done a lot of the observing for you. I have experimented, tried, failed, succeeded, and found what consistently works when it comes to meetings.

Your meeting can go from distracted to focused, from too long to just right. And when it does, you'll see people's behaviors magically transform from bullying, negative, or withdrawn to enlivened and contributing. It's really amazing.

It is to you and your sanity that this book is dedicated, because I know you have better things to do. And because you have better things to do, this book is written in a straightforward, focused, specific style, with actionable items—just the way all meetings should be.

I advise that you read this book in the order it is written. Each part of the Meeting Jet process builds on the last and supports the next. Ultimately, everyone involved in your meetings will need a copy of this book so that they can not only understand the process but also be "keepers of the process."

At the end of each chapter is a section titled "Great Moments in Meetings." These are stories my clients have shared or things I've experienced at meetings. After putting in practice the techniques you'll learn, I would love to hear from you, about your own great moments in meetings.

Right now, it begins with you. Are you ready to transform your meetings into focused, productive uses of time? Buckle up and enjoy the flight.

GREAT MOMENTS IN MEETINGS

One Is the Loneliest Number

We have biweekly team meetings to go over the schedules, near-term actions, and open issues. These are held in a large conference room with a long table running down the center. People sit in chairs on both sides of the conference table, as well as in chairs along each side of the room. At each meeting I stand at the front of the room from where I give a high-level program update and then go around the room, asking for updates and roadblocks.

One day, I noticed a team member sitting against the wall, taking notes on his tablet. As I walked around the table, I discovered he was not taking notes but playing solitaire. I grabbed his tablet, plugged it into the projector, and asked the entire team to help him finish the game. Then I ended the meeting.

Little did I know that this action would turn into a meeting urban legend that was repeatedly shared.

—*Program manager, Consumer technology company*

1

Meet the Passengers: Problem Behaviors at Meetings and Their Effects

In the middle of every difficulty lies opportunity.
—ALBERT EINSTEIN

Let's begin by looking at what we are up against with people. Given that most have too much to do and feel that half their time in meetings is a waste, they may already be in their stress response at a meeting. The problem behaviors people tend to exhibit when they are under stress are described in the book I cowrote with Dr. Rick Kirschner, *Dealing with People You Can't Stand: How to Bring Out the Best in People at Their Worst*. In it, we emphasized that to be effective in bringing out the best in others, it is more function-ally effective to think in terms of behavior rather than personality.

Personality is just a generalization we make based on the behaviors we observe in others. People's behaviors change according to context (where they are and what is going on) and relationship (who they are with). You can know someone who seems to be a bully most of the time, but you may not realize what a wimp that person can be in a different context or a different relationship. My wife will tell you that she has to come to a seminar to hear me speak because in most social situations I'm pretty quiet.

Virtually all parents have experienced their child's coming back from a play date and being surprised to hear the other parent say, "Oh, your child is so polite and helpful!" Different contexts, different behaviors; different relationships, different behaviors.

The reason this is critical to keep in mind is that we as human beings can pay attention to only seven, give or take two, things at any one time consciously. We have a part of our brainstem called the *reticular activating system*, or RAS for short. One of its many functions is radar. If you get married, you suddenly see everyone getting married. If you are having a baby, it looks like a baby boom. If you are interested in a certain car, you start seeing it everywhere. If you think somebody's personality is negative, guess what you notice? You become consciously aware of all the times they're negative and ignore any evidence when they're not.

This is why it's more effective to think in terms of behavior, because then you pay attention in the here and now to what's going on in this context and relationship, and ultimately, you will be more effective. Think of it like clothing. Depending on where you're going and the weather, you wear different outfits. A meeting is a specific context that seems to bring out the worst in people.

If meetings aren't organized and are a waste of time, people are more likely to go into their stress behaviors. To make matters worse, one stress behavior usually triggers others. For example, if one person at a meeting is being controlling, then someone else who is also assertive might fight for control. As they vie for control, other participants might withdraw and stop contributing altogether or simply go along with whatever the most dominant person wants, never sharing what they really think until after the meeting.

In *Dealing with People You Can't Stand*, we offered a way of organizing and understanding why people act the way they do. It is called the Lens of Understanding. The good news is that when you understand why people act the way they do at meetings, it's the first step to understanding what to do about it. And the better news is that when you implement the process in this book—which I have tested and used for the last 20 years—you will prevent all these difficult behaviors from ever occurring. Really. I'm not kidding.

THE COOPERATION ZONE

Let's take a look at the Lens of Understanding (Figure 1.1). Caution: this is *not* personality typing but behavior typing. All of us are capable of all these behaviors to varying degrees, depending on context and relationship. In this chapter, we are focused on behaviors created specifically in the meeting context.

In the center we have a Cooperation Zone. When people are in that zone, there are no problems. And all people have within them four basic intents:

- *Get it done*

- *Get it right*

- *Get along*

- *Get appreciated*

Depending on context (where you are and what's going on) and relationship (who you are with), one of these intents becomes primary, and behavior moves in that direction.

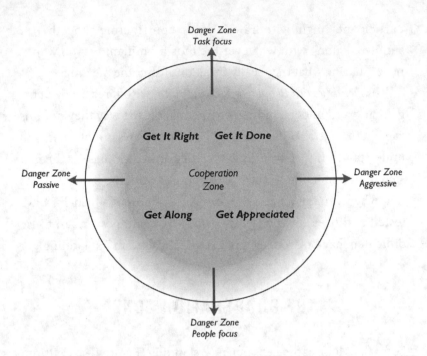

FIGURE 1.1 The Cooperation Zone

When people are in a *Get it done* mode, their behavior becomes focused on the task at hand and more assertive as they push forward to make it happen.

When people are in a *Get it right* mode, they remain focused on the task, but they tend to be less assertive as they slow things down to make sure it is done correctly.

When people are in a *Get along* mode, they are people focused and tend to be more passive, yielding to others and considering the needs of others above their own.

And when people are in a *Get appreciated* mode, they are people focused because that is where appreciation comes from. They become more assertive as they try to contribute to others to receive appreciation.

THE CAUTION ZONE

If people are not getting what they need in a particular situation, they enter the Caution Zone, where their behavior becomes a bit extreme (Figure 1.2). So if people are in a *Get it done* mode and they see things are not happening, they tend to get more *Controlling*. They take over in an effort to *Get it done*.

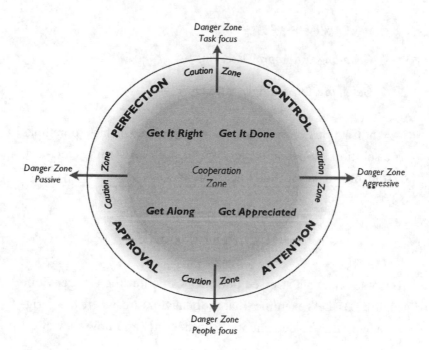

FIGURE 1.2 The Caution Zone

When people are in a *Get it right* mode and they perceive others are not paying enough attention to the details, they compensate by becoming more *Perfectionist*.

If people are in a *Get along* mode but they are worried about potential conflict or the disapproval of others, their behavior becomes more *Approval seeking*.

And if people are in a *Get appreciated* mode and they feel others aren't paying attention to them, their behavior becomes more *Attention seeking*.

As you begin to pay closer attention to people's behaviors at meetings, you will notice how they communicate and act out of these intents and behaviors:

> *Get it done* and *Controlling*
>
> *Get it right* and *Perfectionist*
>
> *Get along* and *Approval seeking*
>
> *Get appreciated* and *Attention seeking*

The Caution Zone is not necessarily a problem. In fact, sometimes it's a solution. Somebody takes control and moves things forward, or someone makes sure all the details are covered.

THE DANGER ZONE

If people really get stressed out, they can enter the Danger Zone (Figure 1.3). Let's examine what the behaviors are, where they originate, why they're detrimental to a meeting, and how they affect others.

Originating out of a desire to *Get it done* and *Control*, we find the behaviors of Tank, Sniper, and Know-it-all.

Tanks

When people become Tanks, they will interrupt, dominate, and roll over others with their point of view. They may even make a direct attack. Tank behavior originates from a desire to *Get it done* and keep things under *Control*. People become Tanks when they perceive

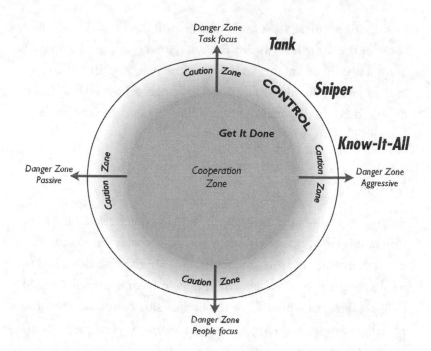

FIGURE 1.3 The Danger Zone: Tanks, Snipers, and Know-It-Alls

that a situation is out of control and/or things are not getting done. They are in such an extreme *Get it done* and *Control* mode that people's feelings are secondary to moving forward, which is why they can be so ruthless. They may attack others personally; ironically, it's nothing personal. They perceive that people stand in the way of a result or are taking too long, so they simply eliminate them.

A Tank's effect at meetings varies according to where others are in the Lens of Understanding, as well as their position in the organization in relation to the Tank. Most, especially subordinates, will simply withdraw and acquiesce to the Tank's point of view, becoming Yes and Nothing People. In the long term they will stop verbally participating at meetings for fear of a Tank attack.

When people suppress anger or resentment, they can easily become Snipers or saboteurs, as we will see. Those subordinates who may harbor resentment about the Tank's behavior are more likely to snipe or perform acts of sabotage behind the Tank's back, while those at the same level as the Tank may make sniping (sarcastic) comments directly at the Tank during the meeting. This of course creates further disruptions. In contrast, a peer who is equally *Get it done* and *Controlling* may opt for an all-out Tank-to-Tank battle in the middle of the meeting.

Snipers

Sniping can take many forms, both verbal and nonverbal, and have different intents, malicious and friendly. *Verbal sniping* is the sarcastic comment, the sarcastic tone, or the barbed jab disguised as a joke. It can also take the form of questions or comments aimed to sabotage a presentation, or it can be a side conversation at the meeting. *Nonverbal sniping* takes the form of facial expressions such as the eye roll or smirk.

Malicious sniping originates from a *Get it done* and *Control* mode. The Sniper has some partially suppressed resentment or anger and can control a meeting by having others live in fear of being shot. *Friendly sniping* originates from a *Get appreciated* and *Attention-seeking* mode. These Snipers may actually like the person at whom they are sniping. Whatever the form, sniping still distracts from the purpose of the meeting by causing a lack of focus. It is also likely that others at the meeting might join in the sniping either by sniping at the snipee (in jest or maliciously) or sniping at the Sniper because they resent the distraction. A Sniper at a meeting can invite a Tank attack because the *Get it done* Tank will be furious at the Sniper for being distracting. Some may simply withdraw and become Nothing People, and others may respond with whining or negativity, if not at the meeting, certainly afterward.

Even if the snipee isn't cut down by the Sniper and is wearing a bulletproof vest in terms of his or her self-esteem, the Sniper's effect on the meeting can be devastating. After a Sniper comment, the others in the room will be focused on the snipee (thinking, "What will she do next?"), the sniper ("What will he do next?"), and themselves ("What would I do in that situation?"). Basically, everyone's attention is somewhere else. Once sniping starts, focus at the meeting is over.

Know-It-Alls

Know-it-all behavior originates from a *Get it done* and *Control* mode. Know-it-alls are very knowledgeable and use their knowledge to control things at a meeting. Although task focused, they are not as task focused as Tanks. When you combine knowledge with a big ego, you get a Know-it-all who will go on and on, dominating the meeting. Maybe they do know 95 percent of a particular subject, but if we remove only 5 percent of the parts of an airplane, are you ready to go for a flight? Of course not! Even if others at a meeting have only 5 percent to contribute, that 5 percent is important. But because Know-it-alls can be intimidating and condescending with their knowledge, most people at a meeting will give up trying to express themselves and simply turn into Nothing People. Know-it-all behavior is detrimental to meetings in two ways: they waste time with their pontificating, and they shut others down.

Let's move to another area of the Lens of Understanding in which people want to *Get appreciated* and they develop a need for attention (Figure 1.4). This produces the behaviors of Think-they-know-it-alls, Grenades, and Friendly Snipers.

Think-They-Know-It-Alls

This behavior can be even more frustrating because they act like Know-it-alls, but they really don't know what they are talking about. It originates from a *Get appreciated* and *Attention-seeking*

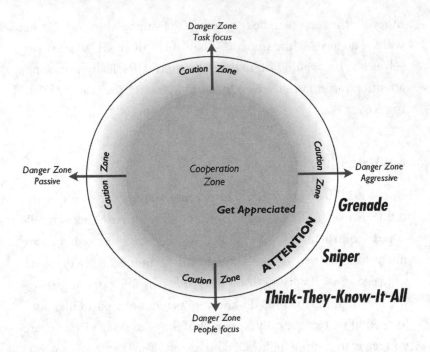

FIGURE 1.4 The Danger Zone: Grenades, Think-They-Know-It-Alls, and Friendly Snipers

mode. They have an even greater ego need to be the center of attention than Know-it-alls have.

They are detrimental to meetings in two ways. First, they waste time going on and on to hear themselves talk. Second, they can mislead a group with bad ideas. If others don't know the subject that Think-they-know-it-alls are talking about, it's easy to follow them off a cliff and into the sea. They can easily trigger a Tank attack or cause in others the sudden need to check their e-mail on their phones for something to do.

Grenades

This behavior is the classic tantrum. It originates from a *Get Appreciated* and *Attention-seeking* mode. They have bottled up a lot of stress, and then their pin is pulled. Often it is because they feel they are not being listened to or their contribution is not being appreciated. Once the tantrum starts, everything else stops. The meeting has really ended. The disruption of the Grenade would infuriate anyone who wants to get things done, so this easily turns other people into Tanks.

When a Tank attacks a Grenade, it is like pouring gasoline on a fire. In the face of a Grenade tantrum, most run for cover by withdrawing and becoming Nothing People. A long-term effect of having Grenades at meetings is that people walk on eggshells around them and are a little more withdrawn. But this can make it more likely for a Grenade to blow up again because when people are withdrawn, they don't give the Grenade the level of attention the Grenade seeks.

Friendly Snipers

Friendly sniping at its nicest can be lighthearted teasing or put-down humor. It's not really meant to hurt anyone, and Friendly Snipers truly are just kidding. It originates from a *Get appreciated* and *Attention-seeking* mode. The teasing is a way of making a connection. However, in the context of a meeting, it is still a distraction. And yes, a joke can lighten up a meeting, but when it's at the expense of another person or happens frequently, it is a distraction. It can easily push *Get it done* people to become Tanks because all sniping is a distraction. Worse, it can be contagious, with others becoming Friendly Snipers too. It may be good for a few laughs, but the focus at the meeting is fractured.

Let's examine another area of the Lens of Understanding in which people want to *Get it right* and develop a need for perfection (Figure 1.5). This produces the behaviors of Whiners, No People, Judges, and Nothing People.

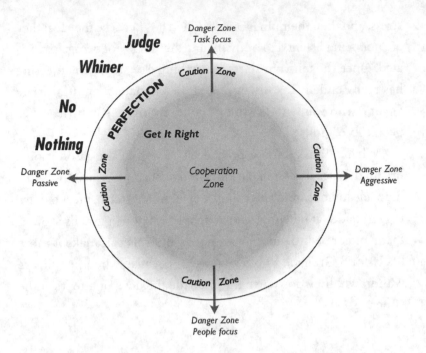

FIGURE 1.5 The Danger Zone: Whiners, No People, Judges, and Nothing People

Whiners

Whining begins in the *Get it right* and *Perfection* mode. They see what could be, compare it with what is, and then feel helpless to do anything about it. At its root, whining comes from feelings of helplessness and disempowerment. Whiners feel they are the victims of other people and circumstances. Then two things happen. Whiners look only at what is wrong with ideas and dismiss them with generalizations such as "Nothing is right," "Everything is wrong," and "It is always that way." Since looking at the specifics of problems is the first step to problem solving, they offer nothing of constructive value.

The Whiner's complaining eventually deflates everyone else at the meeting, robbing them of their energy and creativity. Unfortunately, whining is contagious. It can spread like the flu through a team, and before you know it, everyone at the meeting is doing it.

No People

This is negativity at its worst. It also originates from the *Get it right* and *Perfection* mode. No People are first cousins to Whiners. Whereas Whiners are helpless, No People are hopeless. They are very sure of their negative opinions and, therefore, are more aggressive about spreading the doom and gloom.

No People shoot down ideas before they have a chance to take flight. Like Whiners, they tend to speak in broad generalizations about everything being wrong, but with even more confidence and conviction. They have the arrogance of a Know-it-all seduced by the dark side of the force. Negativity is also a virulent behavior. It will sap the creativity and energy of everyone at the meeting. Of course, No People won't think they did anything wrong. Their motto is, "I'm not being negative. I'm being realistic!"

Judges

While Whiners and No People speak in generalizations, Judges focus on what's wrong by nitpicking the details. They too originate from the *Get it right* and *Perfection* mode. At a meeting, Judges will be overly focused on details that may not be significant or even meaningful to the discussion. Their net result at a meeting is to waste time and take the group down unnecessary tangents. This can easily trigger anyone in the *Get it done* mode while compelling others to withdraw in quiet misery.

Nothing People

These are the people who simply say nothing. Their behavior originates from *Get it right* and *Perfectionist* frustration. They give up and say, "Fine, do it your way, but don't come crying to me when it doesn't work out."

However, there is a type of Nothing People that originates from the *Get Along* and *Approval-seeking* area of the Lens of Understanding (Figure 1.6) who believe that if you don't have something nice to say, don't say it at all. In this area you also get Yes People who are agreeable but you don't know where they stand and Maybe People who can't make a decision.

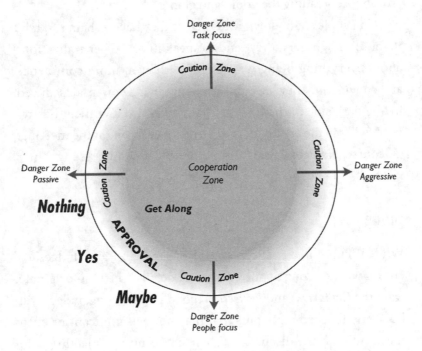

FIGURE 1.6 The Danger Zone: Nothing People, Yes People, and Maybe People

No matter what the motivation for Nothing behavior, *Get it right* and *Perfectionist* or *Get along* and *Approval seeking*, you never hear from them at meetings. They do not participate, and you don't know where they stand. One detriment to the meeting is that their valuable contributions are lost. Another is that they can become passive-aggressive and later engage in sabotage because they didn't agree with the decisions made. After the meeting, they can also easily become Whiners or No People because they feel like victims of decisions that they had a chance to affect but did not.

Therefore, their detriment to the meeting is threefold. One, they simply don't contribute; two, they can become passive-aggressive; and three, they create a wide open space where some of the more assertive behaviors of Tanks, Snipers, and Know-it-alls can dominate.

Yes People

Yes behavior originates from a *Get along* and *Approval-seeking* mode. The last thing they want is to make waves. They will avoid conflict at all costs by suppressing their true feelings and just going along with everyone else. This creates two detriments at a meeting. One is the loss of their valuable contribution or perspective. The other is that when they disagree with decisions made at the meeting, they don't give voice to it. This can lead to passive-aggressive behavior as they engage in subtle acts of sabotage or sniping afterward because of their resentment.

Yes People may also feel like victims, which can turn them into Whiners or No People. Feeling helpless is the root of whining, whereas feeling hopeless is the root of negativity. At the meeting, they are happy to yield the floor to the more assertive behaviors, allowing those people and their opinions to dominate.

Maybe People

Maybe behavior also originates from a *Get along* and *Approval-seeking* mode. This is essentially a Yes Person faced with making a decision that could hurt someone's feelings. Since Maybe People don't want to do that, they will stall and put the decision off until it is too late. Then the decision is made by default and they are not to blame. At meetings, if a boss who is the final decision-maker or too many participants become Maybe People, it will lead to multiple meetings on the same topic as the group recycles discussions and information that it should have acted on long ago.

Every one of these Danger Zone behaviors will quickly destroy a meeting (Figure 1.7). To make matters worse, each Danger Zone behavior tends to trigger Danger Zone behaviors in others.

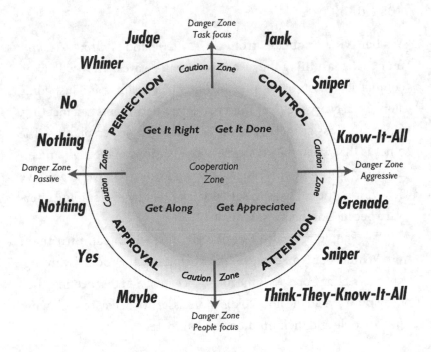

FIGURE 1.7 The Danger Zone Composite

After the meeting, it will only get worse because if people feel that their time was wasted, they will go into some other stress behavior. They might switch into *Get it done* mode and exhibit Tank behavior. Or if they react by feeling helpless or hopeless, they might turn into Whiners and No People who spread their misery to others who weren't even at the meeting.

Here's the good news: with the Meeting Jet process, I'll show you how you can prevent all of these behaviors from occurring in the context of a meeting. If you need surefire strategies to pull people out of these difficult behaviors and prevent them in the first place in other contexts and relationships, please read *Dealing with People You Can't Stand*.

GREAT MOMENTS IN MEETINGS

The Old Have-to-Pee Trick

Back in the 1990s I worked for a well-known telecom R&D lab that had purchased your *Difficult People* videos. At the time, I worked with a Grenade. This particular engineer would explode at any time for seemingly any reason. During one particular design meeting, he was doing his usual ranting and raving. I really needed to use the restroom, so I just got up and left the meeting without explanation.

When I returned, another engineer pulled me aside and told me that my approach was masterful. What approach? The Grenade assumed that I had walked out in silent protest of his behavior. He instantly reformed and became useful. My implied rebuke apparently sobered him, much to my amazement.

—*Engineer, Telecom R&D lab*

SUMMARY

1. People's behaviors change according to context and relationship.

- Context = where they are and what is going on

- Relationship = who they are with

2. *The Cooperation Zone:* Everyone has four basic intents, and whichever is foremost at the time affects their behavior.

    - *Get it done* = task focus and assertive

    - *Get it right* = task focus and passive

    - *Get along* = people focus and passive

    - *Get appreciated* = people focus and assertive

3. *The Caution Zone:* If people are not getting what they need, they go into the Caution Zone, which is not always a problem and is sometimes a solution.

    - *Get it done* = task focus and assertive become *Controlling*

    - *Get it right* = task focus and passive become *Perfectionist*

    - *Get along* = people focus and passive become *Approval seeking*

    - *Get appreciated* = people focus and assertive become *Attention seeking*

4. *The Danger Zone:* If people get really stressed out, they go into the Danger Zone.

    - *Get it done* = task focus and assertive become *Controlling*

        o Tanks

        o Snipers

        o Know-it-alls

- *Get appreciated* = people focus and assertive become *Attention-seeking*

  o Think-they-know-it-alls

  o Friendly Snipers

  o Grenades

- *Get it right* = task focus and passive become *Perfectionist*

  o Whiners

  o No People

  o Judges

  o Nothing People

- *Get along* = people focus and passive become *Approval-seeking*

  o Nothing People

  o Yes People

  o Maybe People

2

Holographic Thinking

E pluribus unum (Out of many, one)
—MOTTO ON THE GREAT SEAL OF
THE UNITED STATES

THE GOAL OF HOLOGRAPHIC THINKING

In my experience everyone at a meeting has something of value to contribute, and when you put it all together, you get something greater. Take your index finger and put it six inches in front of your nose. Close your right eye and look at your finger. Now open it and close your left eye and look at your finger. Now go back and forth a few times: right eye, left eye, right eye, left eye. Isn't it incredible that your finger seems to move? Each of your eyes sees from a different

31

point of view. Imagine them arguing over whose point of view is correct—which is absurd because they are both correct. When your brain puts the two different points together, it allows you to see in three dimensions.

Everyone is right from his or her point of view because, by definition, a point of view is limited. It includes only so much and leaves a lot out. Just as the integration of the unique points of view of your two eyes enables you to see in three dimensions, the integration of people's different points of view on any subject creates what I call Holographic Thinking. When groups get to a Holographic Thinking state, they arrive at an understanding of the subject that is greater and more detailed and that takes into account more factors than any one person can be aware of. Holographic Thinking produces higher-quality ideas and solutions. And it does so quickly, so you can meet less and do more.

The uniqueness of people's points of view is based on their personal life experience, their professional orientation, and where they might be in the Lens of Understanding. For example, a pharmaceutical company I have worked with has meetings to discuss a new drug. Scientists, marketing people, administrators, and lawyers attend these meetings. These people look at the drug differently based on their professional orientations.

The more quickly and more completely you get everyone in a meeting to see everyone else's point of view, the better able you will be to avoid conflict and generate higher-quality ideas that are inclusive of many factors. Differing points of view and unwillingness to integrate them are one of the major sources of conflict at meetings. When a process is in place that integrates points of view, it bypasses conflict and misunderstanding, which in turn makes meetings shorter, more productive, and even fun.

I was on the board of directors of a national association. The board was discussing a membership issue. I suggested, "If our customers are not doing business with us, maybe we are not appealing to their needs and we should do a survey to find out what they really want from us."

The executive director, Betsy, said, "That's a great idea!"

I told her I would write a draft survey and get it to her by Friday for her input, and she could send it out the next week.

She was shocked, "Next week!? It will take months to figure out how to do a proper survey and months to do the statistical analysis."

I said, "Months!? We needed this information at the last board meeting. You are describing a process that will take us beyond the next board meeting."

Notice that we are looking at performing the survey from two different points of view. In terms of the Lens of Understanding, I am in *Get it done* mode. "I'll write it up and get it out next week." She is in *Get it right* mode. "Study how to do it properly for months." Whose point of view is correct? They both are. Each of us can easily make a convincing logical case as to the need to have the information quickly or the need to make sure it is done accurately.

If we have no flexibility to understand each other, we both go into our stress behaviors, trying to convince the other and/or the group as to the rightness of our point of view. That can lead to an argument, which is really nothing more than two people simultaneously thinking they are right and needing very badly to be understood, but at that moment no one is able to do it. Doing that over a period of time leads to polarization, in which you start with the premise that you are right to the exclusion of other points of view, which you automatically oppose.

Meetings can quickly degenerate into camps of your allies and adversaries over contentious issues. If someone "wins" by getting the group to vote according to his or her point of view, it will be at the expense of others. Perhaps I could have persuaded the board to move forward quickly, but some of the important details that Betsy was paying attention to would be lost—not to mention how

Betsy might feel about my power play with the board and how that will affect our future interactions together.

But wait, there's more. Passive people at a meeting may resent the assertive people for pushing their point of view, but they aren't willing to fight for what they believe. And though the "winners" may have gotten their way this time, they will be made to pay later as the "losing" side doesn't get mad but gets even.

In the example of the board of directors, the hologram about the survey comes from finding a balance between *Get it done* and *Get it right* through the integration of the differing points of view. Thankfully, we both had enough consciousness and flexibility to know this. Betsy said, "You're right, we can't wait months for this information." And I said, "You're right, if we are going to invest our time and resources, we'd better do it correctly." Now you have two people approaching an issue from different points of view not as adversaries but as allies. Betsy agreed that it needed to be done before the next board meeting in six weeks. I agreed with her that it needed to be done properly. We wasted no time in polarization and owned both intentions. That freed our energy and focus to figure out a way to do it correctly in the necessary time frame. I was pushing it forward, and she was making sure all details were covered. Because we approached it as team members, we got it done right, and the survey was a success.

If you think of this like a team sport, depending on the position you play, you have different primary responsibilities. One person's primary responsibility may be defense (as a goalie) whereas another's is offense (as a forward), but they are both on the same team and in it together. Each is playing his or her part to the best of his or her ability. When integrated with team members doing the same, this produces a winning result.

So it is with people at meetings. As time went on with the board of directors, I usually played the *Get it done* position and Betsy played the *Get it right* position, making sure all the important details were covered. However, every once in a while, on a particular subject, we would completely reverse roles, and I would be the one paying attention to the details while she drove it forward. What that produced was an effective team that could get things done right!

If people polarize in adversarial stances, the consequences are the following:

1. Conflict at the meeting.

2. Wasted time in arguments in which people take positions instead of seeking solutions.

3. Resentment from those with the "losing" point of view, which can create more conflict at future meetings.

4. Some people withdrawing and no longer being willing to contribute.

5. The meeting will not produce the highest-quality ideas and outcomes.

Can you say gridlock?

In contrast, if you make the assumption that people are right from their respective points of view and if you have a process to genuinely understand and integrate each other's point of view, you will accomplish the following:

1. Avoid conflict

2. Save time

3. Experience better teamwork and harmony

4. Encourage greater contributions from team members

5. Generate higher-quality ideas and outcomes

CREATING THE HOLOGRAM

Creating the hologram will require the following:

1. Eliminating competition to speak so that everyone participates

2. Having everyone focused on the same topic at the same time, using the same process (that is, brainstorming, discussing, and looking at the pros or cons)

3. Paying attention to time for each agenda item, including what's allocated for speaking

4. Visually recording people's contributions to see the big picture and facilitate Holographic Thinking

The first thing you must do is make it easy for people to express themselves without competition to be heard, and you must minimize the potential for stress behaviors. Divide people into two categories at meetings: those who will do whatever it takes to express themselves and those who will not bother. As you saw in the Lens of Understanding, those who will do what it takes can be, at worst, loud, emotional, constantly interrupting, or dominating, or they will simply go on and on. Those who don't bother say absolutely nothing, just say yes, or simply go along with whatever everyone else wants. Either way, you do not have the third dimension. You automatically lose the hologram if people compete to be heard or withdraw.

Next, you need to keep everyone focused on the same topic, using the same process. You must pay attention to the amount of time people are allowed to speak and make sure each topic and process has its allotted time. Everyone is on the flight together, and paying attention to focus and time prevents the meeting from straying off course or arriving at its destination (end) late.

Finally, you need to have visual recording, such as a flip chart or computer-projector combination, which will facilitate Holographic Thinking, as well as support successful follow-up.

In the subsequent chapters, I'll show you in detail how to accomplish all of this and create a great Holographic Thinking team during the meeting. But before we can take off, we need to make a Flight Plan.

GREAT MOMENTS IN MEETINGS

The Greater Rick

In my writing partnership and friendship with Dr. Rick Kirschner, we used to get into all kinds of conflict over our points of view. Sometimes we would even convince each other at the same time of the other's point of view, switch points of view, and argue that too. Eventually, we would end up with an integration of our points of view that produced something better than either of us would have come up with alone. It took a lot of time and trouble until we learned how to get into a Holographic Thinking mindset.

We started operating on the assumption that both of us were right from our respective points of view and each of us had a part of the puzzle. We assumed that when we integrated our pieces, we would have something greater. When we did that, we called our combined selves "the Greater Rick." We would begin a meeting by asking, "Will the Greater Rick please come into the room?" Then we were both eager to hear the other's point of view, put them together in Holographic Thinking, and voilà! It worked, and the result was the book *Dealing with People You Can't Stand.*

When I shared this with a company whose initials were ET, the meeting participants started to begin all meetings with, "Will the Greater ET please come into the room?" Everyone would laugh and be reminded that they were part of a greater team. It led to curiosity about each other's point of view and asking questions to make sure they understood it fully before responding. It also resulted in people asking those who had not yet spoken on the topic what their thoughts were.

—*Dr. Rick Brinkman*

SUMMARY

1. Everyone is "right" from his or her point of view, but a point of view is limited.

2. The uniqueness of people's point of view is based on their personal life experience, their professional orientation, and where they might be in the Lens of Understanding.

3. Holographic Thinking comes from getting everyone to contribute and understand each other's point of view.

4. Polarization is the opposite. It's when people think they are right, to the exclusion of other points of view.

5. Creating the hologram requires the following:

   - Eliminating competition to speak so that everyone participates

   - Everyone is focused on the same topic at the same time, using the same process (that is, brainstorming, discussing, looking at pros or cons)

   - Paying attention to time for speaking and each agenda item

   - Making a visual recording to enable everyone to see the big picture and to facilitate Holographic Thinking

6. By engaging in Holographic Thinking, you achieve the following:

- Avoid conflict

- Save time

- Experience better teamwork and harmony

- Encourage greater contributions from team members

- Generate higher-quality ideas and outcomes

PART II

BEFORE *the*

MEETING

3

Preparing for a Meeting: Your Preflight Checklist

Meetings: where minutes are kept and hours are lost.
—Anonymous

What precedes an effective meeting with Holographic Thinking is preparation. Preparation begins with the preflight checklist:

Preflight Checklist

1. Question the meeting's existence.

2. Count the cost.

3. Decide on the right format.

4. Consider who really needs to be there.

5. Create the agenda.

1. QUESTION THE MEETING'S EXISTENCE

What's the real purpose of the meeting, and is it best served by meeting? Never presuppose that you should be meeting in the first place. Before holding a meeting, always question its necessity. Evaluate if the meeting should exist by asking the following questions:

- What is the purpose of this meeting?

- Is a meeting the right format to accomplish the purpose?

- Can the purpose be accomplished in a better way?

Some meetings are held simply because they always have been. I was reviewing the current meetings at one company and found that nothing substantial was being accomplished at a long-standing weekly meeting. They were reporting information to each other that was actually better done in writing. When I suggested the meeting be eliminated, their response was, "Oh, but that is the only time we all have to get together." What they really wanted was an opportunity to feel like a team and foster connections among people.

Perhaps at one time, the sharing of information at the meeting was a valid purpose, but with the advent of other technologies, the purpose had diminished. However, as people got busier and had less time to interact, the secondary purpose of feeling like a team developed. Once everyone agreed that the real purpose for this meeting was to get everyone together, they eliminated the false purpose of passing on information and organized the meeting in a way that supported its real purpose.

The meeting would start informally with refreshments while people stood around chatting. Once they sat down, they went around the room in circular order, and everyone had two minutes to share whatever was going on with them. It could be about what they were working on, asking for help with something, or how their kitchen remodel was overwhelming their life. The mission of feeling like a team was accomplished even better than before.

The Only Legitimate Reason to Hold a Meeting

Although there are many motives for having a meeting, there is only one legitimate reason: meetings are for interaction. In successful meetings, information may be presented. However, it is interacted upon via discussion, brainstorming, questioning, and so on. Interaction of some sort is a necessary component of every great meeting. When it is time for people to interact on a particular subject, it is time for a meeting.

The Reason Not to Meet

Meetings are not the best vehicle for merely presenting information. Human beings need time to understand, digest, and absorb information.

The Cambridge Psychological Society found that the average person, 24 hours after a business meeting, remembers only 9 percent of what was said, and of the 9 percent remembered, half of it is inaccurate. Part of the reason for this poor recollection is that people have a limited amount of attention. It has been found that human beings can consciously be aware of seven (plus or minus two) things at any one time. Check it out right now. What are you aware of? You could be aware of this book, the feelings in your body, the thoughts that you are thinking, the temperature in the room, and any sounds around you. But if you suddenly hear a CRASH, your attention will go to that sound, and something you were consciously aware of a moment ago will drop out.

At meetings, people are not 100 percent consciously focused on the information being presented at every single moment. Certain pieces of information may stimulate them into thought. Those thoughts may or may not be relevant to the information being presented. One meeting participant might be considering the morale implications of what was just said, which actually may be important to the discussion. At the same time another participant, through the magic of free association, just remembered something that needs to be picked up on the way home. Either way, while their conscious attention is distracted, they are missing more incoming information.

People's attention also can be affected by external distractions, such as noticing two people at the meeting who are having a private conversation. Or their attention can be affected by physical sensations, such as the vibration of their smartphone or the discomfort of their chair. Or they might suddenly notice the time, compare it to the agenda, and realize their schedule is toast. That realization alone will certainly set off a whole internal cascade of distracting thoughts.

But the problem with giving information at meetings isn't only people's limited attention. Another factor to consider is that everyone has personal filters through which the information passes and may be transformed into something different from what the presenter intended. Interpretation of words also may vary. You may have noticed that certain words mean different things to different people. That also will affect the interpretation of information. People may be listening to information from different points of view, such as what's wrong with an idea, how it will affect the listener, its implications for their budget, and so on. When people are filtering, they are distracted and don't absorb all the information being presented. In turn, partial understanding further alters the meaning made out of the communication.

Yet another factor that gets in the way of receiving and remembering accurate information is that a human being's capacity for short-term memory decreases with age. So no matter how much people try to focus, their ability to remember 24 hours later is affected.

To summarize, the problems with giving information at meetings are these:

- People have a limited amount of attention.

- There are internal and external distractions.

- People have personal filters.

- People have a limited ability to remember.

So let me be crystal clear: having a meeting simply to disseminate information is not a good use of a meeting. Information should be provided as documentation on paper or electronically. When information is documented, everyone has the exact same information. It will be the same tomorrow and a week from now. If you missed something the first time, you can reread it.

If you find yourself attending a meeting for the purpose of giving information with no interaction, you should do everyone a favor and question the existence of that meeting.

What About the Importance of Interacting on Information?

Remember that meetings are for interaction! Therefore, interacting on information is a good use of meeting time. People also may need to ask questions about information to further their understanding. Discussions related to the information may be important. Analyzing options presented in the information may be required.

All of these are good uses of meeting time. However, in this case, it would be best for everyone to have the information ahead of time. Allow the appropriate amount of time to read it and digest it and then come to the meeting ready to ask questions and interact on the information. This ensures higher-quality interaction at the meeting because people have had time to think about and organize their thoughts or questions.

An Exception to the Rule

There may be times when you decide not to put information in writing because you want everyone to hear exactly the same thing, at the same time, in the same way. For example, one company needed to break some bad news to employees. The senior managers did not want anyone in the organization to find out from anyone else through the rumor mill or blow it out of proportion. This was a good use of a meeting because it controlled the timing and delivery of the information.

In general, major news regarding an organization's business is better given at what is sometimes called an "all-hands-meeting" or a "town hall." In this situation, it is usually the most senior person in the organization who is presenting the report. Q&A may be possible, but more often, people afterward break into smaller groups to interact on the information with their direct managers.

I've worked with organizations that usually allowed direct managers to break the bad news to their team members. The problem with that system is you have about 60 direct managers reinterpreting and translating the information they received from senior management. It is very unlikely that 60 direct managers will communicate exactly the same thing in the same way. Some may not have fully understood what senior management was asking them to communicate, but they didn't ask for clarification. Others thought they understood but really didn't. And we can't underestimate the style of their communication.

Appearance and tone are much more significant than the words said. The communicators' tone of voice and whether they appear matter of fact, empathetic, unsympathetic, or some other way will make or break the communication. In general, it is best for bad news to come from the top and then have the direct managers interact with their team members about it. That way, the team members will feel that they are in it together with their managers. They will have an easier time discussing what the news means to them and how to deal with it.

Another exception for using a meeting to present information is if you need to see and hear people's initial reactions to the information. You may not have the same level of quality questions you would if people had a chance to think about it, but experiencing their initial reactions qualifies as interaction and so is a good use of meeting time. However, in this case, it would be wise to have whatever information is presented also distributed in document form at the meeting so that people can refer to it later.

2. COUNT THE COST

No meeting is free. I met some folks at a British company that installed computers in each of the meeting rooms. When you arrived, you keyed in your code. The computer knew what you were paid per minute, and as the meeting ran, a taxi meter appeared on the screen showing the total cost. That awareness cut their meeting times in half.

But there is more than the direct cost of what people are paid to consider. There is the cost of people's time. How about all the tasks people are not doing while they're at the meeting? This calculation is called the *time/benefit ratio*. Is the amount of time spent on this meeting worth the benefit that results from the meeting? This calculation is important in three ways: the decision to hold a meeting, deciding who really needs to be at the meeting, and deciding what topics are put on the agenda.

3. DECIDE ON THE RIGHT FORMAT

Start by considering if a face-to-face meeting is best or if the purpose of the meeting can be accomplished via a virtual meeting. Sometimes the geographic distances between people make it cost ineffective for them to meet face-to-face. Other times the topics that need to be discussed are so complex or hot or lengthy that a face-to-face meeting is the way to go. You also may have the secondary objective of wanting people to bond as a team. If this is the case, then make it a live meeting.

We will talk about virtual meetings in great detail in Chapter 12. For now, let me say that in a virtual meeting you should always ensure that participants can see a shared screen. In general, avoid audio-only conference calls or people calling into a virtual meeting but not seeing a shared screen on their computers.

You also may want to consider a meeting in which webcams are turned on. This immediately accomplishes two things:

1. It will give people a feeling of connection.

2. It will create accountability to stay focused and eliminate multitasking.

Some meetings will be a mix of face-to-face and virtual, as when groups of people are in rooms together in different geographic locations—for example, Hong Kong, London, and New York.

4. CONSIDER WHO REALLY NEEDS TO BE THERE

The attendee list is critical. Each agenda item must relate to everyone who is there. What happens if you have 10 people at a meeting but one of the agenda items concerns only 6 of them? You have 4 bored people who will naturally look for a diversion, such as having a side conversation, checking their phones, or engaging in other distracting behaviors. Having people attend who are not involved in an agenda item dilutes the energy of the meeting. It is better to have only the people who are really involved in each agenda item.

Make sure you have all the right people. If a decision must be made but all the necessary people can't be there, then reschedule the meeting for when everyone can attend.

Get More Done with Less

You want the least number of people that can completely fulfill the purpose of the meeting. The more attendees at the meeting, the harder it will be for everyone to speak or to go back and forth in a discussion on a subject. There is also an increased likelihood of distraction and misunderstanding. This is illustrated by the *communication pathways formula*. A *communication path* is a one-way direction between one person and another. So two people have two communication paths between them, one coming to a person, the other going from that person. Every communication path at a meeting is an opportunity for distraction and misunderstanding.

The communication pathways formula is $x(x-1)$ = number of communication pathways at the meeting, where x equals the number of people at the meeting.

If you have a five-person meeting, you have 20 communication pathways, $5(5-1) = 20$. Adding one person to the meeting increases it to 30 communication pathways, $6(6 - 1) = 30$. The difference between 20 pathways and 30 pathways is 10. Ten is 50 percent of the 20 pathways you had at the five-person meeting. Therefore, by adding just one person to the meeting you increased the opportunity for distraction and misunderstanding by 50 percent.

When in doubt, leave them out. If you are worried about offending people, offer them the choice to opt out and get notes later. Most will be more than happy to opt out.

Doers and Deciders, Resource People, and Need-to-Know People

I have found that often the reason for having too many people at a meeting is that there is no conscious awareness of the three types of people:

1. **Doers and deciders:** These are the people who are taking action on a project and are actively making decisions related to it. Sometimes the doer and the decider are two different people, as when a doer reports to someone higher up in the organization who ultimately makes the decision. Or the doer might be given authority to be a decider within certain limitations but goes to the higher-up for decisions that exceed the delegated authority. Other times they are one person.

2. **Resource people:** These are people who have the skills, experience, and perspectives that can support the project, but they are not actively doing or deciding things.

3. **Need-to-know people:** They are not doing or deciding. Neither are they contributing resources, but they need to know what is going on.

I consulted with a board of directors on a project I was asked to lead. The task was to study their process for getting things done and help them make their committees functional. My goal was to form a model committee and learn what it would take to reach a level of functioning that would be productive. At the board meeting, they asked me what I needed. I told them I wanted a core of five people, and I named one of them. Before I could go any further, I was cut off by one board member. (They were not using my process. No one should ever be able to cut off a speaker unless the speaker is over his or her allotted time. See Chapter 8, "Balancing Participation with Air Traffic Control.")

That board member was the speaker of the house. He promptly named himself, the president, the president-elect, and the executive director to the committee. In addition, he wanted time to choose an additional 5 people personally. When all was said and done, my 5-person team became an 11-person team. Worse, I knew all the officers he named didn't have time for it. To make matters worse, it took him over two months to choose the additional people, which translated into two months of inaction. Once we finally had everyone on the committee, it immediately became completely nonfunctional because, even using online scheduling software and scanning a three-month period, we could not find a single time when we could all meet.

The moral of this story is twofold:

1. If you hire consultants, you probably should listen to them.

2. Too many people is often worse than too few.

The reason the committee bloated to 11 was because no distinction was made among doers and deciders, resource people, and need-to-know people.

Most of those named—the president, president-elect, speaker, and executive director—were in the resource or need-to-know category. In fact, of the 11, the only doers were me and the person I got to choose. And I chose him because I knew he had both the skills needed to do the job and the time to do it.

I recommend that on any project you clearly identify who the doers, deciders, resource people, and need-to-know people are. The resource and need-to-know people should be kept in the loop on e-mails, and they should receive summaries of meetings. That way, if the resource people have something to add, they are up-to-date and can jump in with a contribution. For example, let's say the doers are going to have a meeting about using social media for marketing. By keeping the resource people aware, the resource person who has expertise in that area can make sure she attends that marketing meeting or chime in via e-mail with important related information. Doers should also know the expertise of their resource people and suggest when their attendance is required.

5. CREATE THE AGENDA

Every meeting must have an agenda. In the Meeting Jet, it's your Flight Plan. A meeting without an agenda is like blowing up a balloon, not tying the end, and then letting it go. It will be a wild ride, and who knows where it will end up. Ideally, the agenda is created and distributed ahead of time.

For spontaneous meetings (you and I meeting in the hall and deciding to take 15 minutes to discuss an issue), the creation of the agenda should be the first item on the agenda. What do we want to accomplish in this 15-minute hall meeting? Decide who will be responsible for creating the agenda, make sure everyone knows the criteria and process to get an item on the agenda, establish a cutoff time for submitting items for the agenda, and decide the ideal point before the meeting to distribute the agenda and any supplementary information people need to prepare themselves. We will go into great detail on this in the next chapter.

A successful meeting begins with careful preparation well before the actual meeting starts. It must have a clear purpose that is best served by the meeting format. A time/benefit analysis should be done in relation to the value of the meeting itself as well as in terms of who should attend. Always remember to consider that while people are spending their time at a meeting, they are not doing all the other tasks clamoring for their attention.

GREAT MOMENTS IN MEETINGS

The Mary Method

For all meetings, we were required to be present only when we were pitching our projects or when our titles were being discussed. An agenda was sent out ahead of time, so everyone knew the order and chronology of the discussion. Our associate publisher, Mary, would e-mail us to let us know when it was time for us to come in. We left as soon as our part of the discussion was over. That way, we didn't have to sit through the rest of the meeting that didn't apply to us or our projects; we could spend that time focused on what we needed to work on. It was a very efficient way to manage the team's time.

—Senior editor, Publishing company

SUMMARY

1. Question the meeting's existence.

- What is the real purpose of this meeting?

- Are we going to interact with each other?

2. Count the cost.

- Is the purpose worth the cost in terms of what people are paid, people's time, and other priorities?

3. Decide on the right format.

- Face-to-face

- Video conference

- Telephone conference

- Mixed face-to-face and remote

4. Consider who really needs to be there.

- What is the time/benefit ratio of each attendee?

- Is each agenda item important to all participants?

- Can we minimize the number of attendees (and communication pathways)?

- Who are the doers, deciders, resource people, and need-to-know people?

5. Create the agenda.

- Who will create the agenda?

- How do people get items on the agenda?

- When will it be done and distributed?

4

The Art of the Agenda:
Your Flight Plan

If you don't know where you are going,
you'll end up someplace else.

—Yogi Berra

A good meeting begins with a clear purpose and an agenda to accomplish that purpose.

If a meeting is spontaneous, the first agenda item is to draw up an agenda. With three coworkers standing in the hall, this can be as simple as stating what the purpose of the informal meeting is and what you hope to accomplish. Ideally, if logistics permit, the informal agenda should be written on a flip chart or whiteboard where everyone can see it. And notes should definitely be taken.

FLIGHT PLAN CHECKLIST

Remember that the goal before a meeting is preparation. The agenda is your Flight Plan for where you want to go and when you want to get there. It is also critical to the success of the goal of focus during the meeting.

1. Who Will Create the Agenda?

This can be one person or a few people. Having one person create the agenda is straightforward and logistically simpler, but there are times when you will want more than one person to be responsible for the agenda. Being the gatekeeper of the agenda is a powerful position. You can decide what gets to the group's attention.

There may be some cases in which having only one person with this responsibility would be giving that person too much power. However, the downsides of having too many people create the agenda are the logistics of getting them together to do it and the time it takes for them to communicate about it and organize it. But even if several people are responsible for creating the agenda, you should always designate only one person to be the recipient of agenda items and information from the other participants and to put together the document.

2. What Is the Process for Submitting Items for the Agenda?

Decide how items should to be sent to the agenda creator—via e-mail, hard copy, or both. Each agenda item submitted must include the following:

1. A topic title

2. A clear purpose (in one or two sentences)—that is, why this item deserves the group's attention

3. Who, if anyone, is taking the lead on this item

4. The processes that will be used (brainstorm, presentation, discussion, and so on)

5. A realistic estimated time frame for the agenda item (that is, 15 minutes for the item, composed of a 5-minute presentation and 10-minute discussion)

6. Any background information attendees will need to read ahead of time

7. What is expected from the group (their opinion, considerations, questions, and so on)

8. Who is doing what and when

3. What Are the Criteria That Make Items Worthy of Being on the Agenda?

Some criteria will vary according to the types of meetings, whereas others will remain consistent. The consistent criteria tend to be similar to the criteria for having a meeting in the first place:

1. The agenda item requires group interaction.

2. The agenda item involves everyone at the meeting.

3. The time/benefit ratio of the item is favorable to including it. The item is worth group time in general, and it is worth the amount of time allotted in relation to the other agenda items that must be covered during the meeting.

Because meetings have a finite amount of time and each agenda item requires a certain amount of time, the people making the agenda must prioritize. This means weighing each item against the others on the agenda and asking, "Is this item worth group time, and if so, how much group time?"

Schedule the most important items first. That way, during the meeting, if you find you need more time for an important item, you can cut less important ones at the end of the agenda.

However, you must always be realistic about time. Do not overschedule in the first place. You may have 10 items that are all important, but realistically, there will be time for only 8 of them. Which get cut? The person or team coordinating the agenda will need to make a judgment call on whether a particular item deserves the group's precious interactive time (or as much as is being requested).

If the agenda creator doesn't think an item deserves the amount of time requested or deserves to be included in the meeting at all, it is a good idea to contact the person who submitted the item by phone or in person, not e-mail. E-mail is too easily misunderstood. When people read an e-mail, they hear it in a certain tone, according to their own stress level, blood sugar, and whatever they have going on at that moment. You don't want to risk having a person feel dissed or dismissed. You need to talk to the person to clarify why the item is important and explore whether it can be handled in another way. Clarification requires interaction. You will waste your time and energy if you do it over e-mail.

In this conversation you might discover that the item's importance was not clear to you in the original submission. If there is not enough time for the item, you might suggest a different way of accomplishing the same result or schedule it for a different meeting.

4. What Is the Deadline for Submitting Agenda Items?

Because we want people to come prepared, they need to receive the agenda and background information related to each item before the meeting. How far ahead of time depends on the volume of the information and its complexity. You don't want to send it too early so that people either read it and forget it or decide to read it later and put it in their inbox, where it gets buried. Neither do you want to send it too close to the meeting so that they don't have time to read it. In general, aim for three to five days ahead of the meeting. It's also a good idea to ask participants what works for them.

Once you have decided how many days ahead of the meeting to distribute the agenda, the next step is to consider how long it will take for you to create the agenda. Distribution time plus creation time are subtracted from the meeting date, and that becomes the deadline for submission of items. If you have a meeting on Friday, May 10, for which you want people to have three days to review the agenda, then distribute the agenda on Tuesday, May 7. If the agenda takes one day to create, you'll do that on Monday, May 6. If you do not include weekends as workdays, then the deadline to submit is Friday, May 3.

I recommend being very strict about the deadline for submitting agenda items and not accepting items after that deadline. Do not reward procrastination. If people like to do things at the last minute, then be clear that the last minute is 5 p.m. on Friday, May 3, and they are welcome to procrastinate to their heart's content until then.

Obviously, it is possible for important things to come up after the deadline that weren't known before but that still need to be addressed at the meeting. It's OK to make an exception for these items. But beware. The majority of things that come up in that time period more often relate to people's poor last-minute work habits and not genuine priorities that first appear in the window between the deadline and the meeting.

During a meeting of a board of directors, some board members distributed background information on paper. I observed the chaos in the room as other board members tried to read what was just given to them while another kept talking. The focus was totally destroyed.

Once my term as president began, I was ruthless and allowed no exceptions. If people didn't submit an agenda item on time, it wasn't getting on the agenda unless I knew the item had genuinely come up in that window between submission and meeting. But there was absolutely no distribution of information allowed at the meeting. All info was due by the agenda deadline. It took only one meeting to get everyone submitting on time, and you know what? They all thanked me for it.

5. Who Will Be Assigned to the Flight Crew?

Some participants at the meeting will also fulfill process roles. We'll go into these roles in great detail in subsequent chapters, but for now they are the Pilot, the Air Traffic Controller, and the Flight Recorder.

The Pilot is the primary timekeeper, keeping the meeting on course and on time. The Air Traffic Controller has two responsibilities. One is to maintain the focus of the group on the current topic and use the current process to keep the meeting on course. The other is to control who can speak such that participation is balanced and assertive people don't dominate and passive people can contribute. The Flight Recorder gathers everyone's points of view in a visual way that facilitates Holographic Thinking and effective follow-up.

THE FORMAT OF YOUR FLIGHT PLAN

Having a workable format for the agenda is as important as having the agenda itself. You want it to be simple to follow but contain all the information you need to keep focused and to navigate the meeting successfully.

On the volunteer boards I have served on, I usually put our vision, mission, and values at the top of the agenda to remind people of our greater purpose. Remember, people can pay attention to only seven things, give or take two. Putting the greater vision in their consciousness is always a good idea.

I also find it useful to give people an overview of what we want to accomplish and what we want to finish when the meeting is done. If you have vision at the top, then this is next. If you don't, then this would be at the top. For example:

What to Achieve at This Meeting

- Reaffirm our vision and mission.

- Review and approve our goals and objectives.

    o What is our legislative plan?

    o How will we increase membership?

- Review and approve the roles of board members for the procedure manual.

- Review the changes in election procedures and bylaws. Formalize that committee.

- Elect new officers.

Each item on the agenda should include the following.

1. The Item Title and Number

This should be specific enough that everyone knows what it means, but it should not be so verbose that it goes on for many lines. For example, "Ramifications of budget cuts" or "Project management issues" or "Status report of XYZ" would be simple and to the point.

Each item should have a number in front of it that represents its order on the agenda. Though the font size for your document may be a standard 10 to 12 points, make the number of the agenda item larger, 16 or 18 points, so it stands out. Then use the regular type and font size for the title of the collateral information that supports that item. This makes it easy for people to find and brief themselves on the collateral information that pertains to the item:

> #3 *Agenda item*: What are the pros and cons of the new move?

2. The Time Frame

At what time will we focus on the item and for how long? Be as accurate as you can. Don't round off. In fact, I highly recommend you use times on the agenda that are not in the usual factor of 5. For example:

> #3 *Agenda item*: What are the pros and cons of the new move?
>
> *Time*: 8:36 to 9:38

This gives the impression that time actually matters (which it does) and that you intend to stick to the schedule. You don't have to be random. Try to be accurate.

How long the group will spend on the item also should be clearly specified:

> #3 *Agenda item*: What are the pros and cons of the new move?
>
> *Time*: 8:36 to 9:38 (62 minutes)

The time frame for each item must be realistic. Here are some factors to consider when setting a time frame:

- How many attendees may want to say something about it?

- How much might they need to say?

- Does this topic require active discussion?

- What is the past history in terms of time required for this topic or this type of topic?

If the amount of time for an agenda item is not realistic, you are setting up the meeting for failure. Knowing the right time frame for each type of item is a learning process; your goal is to get better at it over time. Learn from each meeting by always taking notes on how long an item actually took.

My recommendation is that you initially allow a bit more time than you will need without being excessive. And if you are done early, people will be really impressed. What people have to say on a topic will expand or contract to fill the time allotted to it.

3. The Person Responsible for This Item

Whoever is responsible for an agenda item should be listed with that item:

> #3 *Agenda item*: What are the pros and cons of the new move?
>
> *Time*: 8:36 to 9:38 (62 minutes)
>
> *Who*: Jack and Mary

4. The Purpose of Having This Item on the Agenda

This is huge! Write a sentence or two that tells everyone why this item is worthy of precious meeting time and why it is important for them to be there. This helps people relax and focus on the item and supports a feeling of accomplishment:

#3 *Agenda item*: What are the pros and cons of the new move?

Time: 8:36 to 9:38 (62 minutes)

Who: Jack and Mary

Purpose: Because the new move will disrupt work flow for a week and will affect all departments, it is important that we examine its ramifications.

5. The Processes to Be Used and Who Will Take the Lead

Different agenda items will require different processes. Some items may require only one process, whereas others may require more than one. (We will discuss the meeting processes in detail in Chapter 11.)

For example, you may have an item that will require a presentation, then a question-and-answer period, then a discussion, and then a vote. Another item may simply be a presentation with questions asked as they occur during the presentation. If different people take the lead on different processes, their names should appear next to the process. It is also important that the time frame for each process be specified, as well as more details on the subject itself. For example:

#3 *Agenda item*: What are the pros and cons of the new move?

Time: 8:36 to 9:38 (62 minutes)

Who: Jack and Mary

Purpose: Because the new move will disrupt work flow for a week and will affect all departments, it is important that we examine its ramifications.

Process:

- Presentation on reasons for the move (10 minutes), Jack

- Question and answer (6 minutes)

- Presentation on anticipated effects on work flow (10 minutes), Mary

- Question and answer (6 minutes)

- Discussion on how you see it affecting your work flow (30 minutes)

6. Information That You Need to Read to Brief Yourself Ahead of Time

Along with the agenda, you should attach any other documents with information the participants need to read before the meeting. Make sure the documents are clearly labeled and named according to the agenda item. Some agenda times may not require any background information, in which case specify "no info" in the info area of the agenda. Also, make it clear that part of the Meeting Jet process will be to not catch up latecomers, so reading ahead of time is expected:

> #3 *Agenda item*: What are the pros and cons of the new move?
>
> *Time*: 8:36 to 9:38 (62 minutes)
>
> *Who*: Jack and Mary
>
> *Purpose*: Because the new move will disrupt work flow for a week and will affect all departments, it is important that we examine its ramifications.

Process:

- Presentation on reasons for the move (10 minutes), Jack

- Question and answer (6 minutes)

- Presentation on anticipated effects on work flow (10 minutes), Mary

- Question and answer (6 minutes)

- Discussion on how you see it affecting your workflow (30 minutes)

Info: Read the attached PDF document describing the move and the spreadsheet that shows the exact times certain areas will be nonfunctional.

7. What Is Expected from the Participants in Relation to This Item

It is critical for participants to focus in the right way on the item. For example, you may want the participants' opinions, or their analysis of the positives and negatives, or for them to understand what is going on, or to have their questions answered. The clearer people are on what is expected of them, the more effective, efficient, and focused they will be. This will also support the elimination of irrelevant tangents.

#3 Agenda item: What are the pros and cons of the new move?

Time: 8:36 to 9:38 (62 minutes)

Who: Jack and Mary

Purpose: Because the new move will disrupt work flow for a week and will affect all departments, it is important that we examine its ramifications.

Process:

- Presentation on reasons for the move (10 minutes), Jack

- Question and answer (6 minutes)

- Presentation on anticipated effects on work flow (10 minutes), Mary

- Question and answer (6 minutes)

- Discussion on how you see it affecting your work flow (30 minutes)

Info: Read the attached PDF document describing the move and the spreadsheet that shows the exact times certain areas will be nonfunctional.

What do you need from me: We want you to consider how this move will directly affect you and your department. Considering the projects you have, when is the ideal time to move?

8. Who Will Do What When

This is where you record any decisions, commitments, and actions to be made after the meeting. Be specific. Include names and dates. Effective follow-up begins with everyone knowing who is doing what and when. (For an agenda document template, visit www.DealingWithMeetings.com.)

#3 *Agenda item*: What are the pros and cons of the new move?

Time: 8:36 to 9:38 (62 minutes)

Who: Jack and Mary

Purpose: Because the new move will disrupt work flow for a week and will affect all departments, it is important that we examine its ramifications.

Process:

- Presentation on reasons for the move (10 minutes), Jack

- Question and answer (6 minutes)

- Presentation on anticipated effects on work flow (10 minutes), Mary

- Question and answer (6 minutes)

- Discussion on how you see it affecting your workflow (30 minutes)

Info: Read the attached PDF document describing the move and the spreadsheet that shows the exact times certain areas will be nonfunctional.

What do you need from me: We want you to consider how this move will directly affect you and your department. Considering the projects you have, when is the ideal time to move?

Who is doing what and when: By Friday, everyone will e-mail Yolanda a prioritized list of preferred times for the move.

CONSIDER THE AGENDA ORDER

In time management there is an efficiency principle called *cluster-ing*. It means you put all the parts of one kind of task together and do them all at once. For example, you can group phone calls, a certain type of paperwork, and a category of e-mail. Clustering is a very efficient way to do things because there is an acceleration phase as you become oriented and get up to speed. Then you cruise very efficiently for a while. When you complete the task, there is a deceleration phase. Because of the acceleration/deceleration, you probably can get more done in one uninterrupted hour than you can in five interrupted 15-minute periods even though technically the latter is more time.

Clustering also improves efficiency at a meeting. Think in terms of clustering the way people's attention is focused. This can be accomplished in a number of ways.

Topic

You can cluster a group of topics that relate to one another. For example, you may have a group of items in a row related to budgetary questions. Once people are oriented and thinking about that topic, they will process it more efficiently.

Process

You can cluster according to process—for example, grouping a number of agenda items that require discussions. Once people are in discussion mode, they become efficient, so the agenda can have a number of different topics in a row that require discussion.

Energy and Time of Day

Another factor to consider in ordering items on the agenda is the energy level of the meeting. I'm sure you've experienced higher-energy and lower-energy meetings. The time of day is one important factor. Consider the different energies that might be created at the following times: first thing in the morning, before lunch, a meeting that is running over into people's lunch hour, after lunch, and at the end of the day. Consider what time of day will support the success of the process.

If a meeting is long (a few hours to a full day), you definitely need to consider agenda items in relation to time of day. I was on a board of directors that met for two days each quarter. When it came to the budget, we found there were two timing considerations that supported the success of that tough topic. One, it needed to be discussed first thing in the morning when people were fresh, and two, it was better addressed on the second day, when the participants were used to discussion and in a decisive mindset.

Energy and Topics

Topics also can affect energy, such as the discussion no one wants to have about reducing the budget. In a long meeting, it is especially important to consider energy level as it relates to topics and process. Over the course of the day, people have higher- and lower-energy periods. Let's call the higher-energy period *prime time*. In terms of your meeting, consider what is prime time, the highest-energy period of the meeting, and use that for the agenda items that will require the most thought, brain power, and focus. Also consider which items can easily be tackled in a lower-energy period and organize the agenda accordingly.

Priorities

Another important factor to consider when you create the order of agenda items is their relative priorities. You may want to put the most important items first. That way, if an item really requires more time than was originally planned for in the agenda, you can create more time for it by postponing to another meeting the discussion of the less important items at the end of the agenda.

A successful meeting begins with preparation. The better and more specific the preparation, the more likely you will be successful at achieving the goal of focus during the meeting.

GREAT MOMENTS IN MEETINGS

The Big Short

Just because you have a meeting, it doesn't mean it has to last an hour. We have multiple regular meetings to report statistics and compliance with laboratory standards. We've figured out how to get through most of them in about 35 minutes, leaving everyone more time to do productive work.

Before, a person would bring a piece of paper, read from it, and then add it to the minutes. We didn't know how many reports there were, and we had to listen to those that didn't require anything. The meeting was fraught with anxiety about how it would go on and on.

We all agreed to prepare ahead of time by sending the data to the assistant so the agenda could contain the data that we used to add. That way, if the sections didn't have anything to report we simply acknowledged and moved on. That shortened the meeting from an hour and 15 minutes to about 30 minutes!

—*Chief MD, Pathology and laboratory medicine*

SUMMARY

1. Who will create the agenda?

2. How do people get items on the agenda?

3. When will it be done and distributed?

4. Who is in the Flight Crew?

   - Pilot

   - Air Traffic Controller

   - Flight Recorder

5. Format each agenda item as follows:

   - # Agenda item

   - Time (time range and total time)

   - Who

   - Purpose

   - Process with times

   - Info

   - What do you need from me

   - Who is doing what and when

6. Set realistic time frames for each item and learn from experience:

   - How many attendees may have something to say about it?

   - How much might they need to say?

   - Does this topic require discussion?

- What is the past history in terms of time required for this topic or this type of topic?

7. Consider the agenda order:

   - Cluster by process?

   - Cluster by topic?

8. Consider the energy and time of day.

9. Consider the energy and topic.

10. Consider ordering items by relative priorities.

5

Start on Time!
End on Time!

If you're not early, you're late.
—MILITARY EXPRESSION

How many minutes have you spent at the beginning of a meeting, not meeting but waiting for others to show up? How many others were also waiting, and what are you each worth per minute? Do the math. Didn't you have better things to do?

How many minutes have you spent at the back end of a meeting that is going longer than scheduled and, even worse, going long because one person always has something lengthy to say while another takes everyone down useless tangents? Then you are late for the next meeting you have right after this one, and you become the person whom people are waiting for.

A NEVER-ENDING CYCLE

People tend to resist meetings because so many seem to be a waste of time. For this reason, it is often hard to pull away from whatever else you are doing to go to a meeting. When people wait for late-comers and a meeting does not start on time, it teaches those who came on time a valuable lesson: "Why waste my time by arriving on time?" At the next meeting, they are less likely to show up on time. However, at that next meeting, some of those who showed up late last time do arrive on time, only to wait for the others who are not there. Once again, the meeting begins late and teaches the same lesson to those who might have missed it the first time: "Why come on time and waste my time?" It does not take very long to perpetuate a never-ending cycle.

Being committed to starting and actually ending on time are equally important to keeping a meeting focused. If people know the meeting will start and end on time and they know it is not going to become a black hole that consumes their day, they will be more focused. Everyone is too busy and has too much to do. Respect for one another's time and the precious resource of group time begins with a commitment to start and end promptly. For that to happen, each agenda item must be thoughtfully and realistically scheduled for the right amount of time to accomplish it.

You must break the cycle and begin a new on-time era. You need to get everyone's commitment to that concept. You want everyone to hear everyone else make that commitment. Ideally, it happens in person at a face-to-face meeting. However, it also can be done via a group e-mail. If you are in a meeting and you have everyone in the room together, I suggest going around the room and having everyone say, "I commit to coming on time." If you are making this commitment via e-mail, each person must write that he or she commits and then reply all to the whole group.

What can you do if people do not keep their commitment? There are all kinds of ways to remind people, so let your imagination run wild. I know of many organizations that locked the door at the start of a meeting and did not let anyone else in. You simply missed it, and you weren't caught up. Another group changed the conference rooms and did not leave a note as to where they went. After latecomers tired of wandering the halls, they made sure they were on time for future meetings. Another group established a fine that collected money for a charitable cause. One team got some un-padded folding steel chairs, and if you were late, that was your seat.

Of course it is possible for people to have valid reasons for being late. They could be coming from another meeting that ran late. They may have been delayed by their boss, a customer, a client, or an emergency. This is certainly allowable and forgivable. What you are trying to eliminate is a standing pattern of chronic lateness that is within an individual's control.

NO CATCH-UP

To support this end, I suggest that you do not catch up latecomers on what has been discussed. Catching people up perpetuates lateness. It enables latecomers to be participants despite being late.

What if the latecomer is someone higher up in the organization than everyone else at the meeting? Before implementing this process, you need to create buy-in ahead of time so that the process applies to *everyone* who attends the meeting, including higher-ups.

The process actually enables people to join in and get up to speed quickly without being briefed verbally. You will see how that works in later chapters.

START AT UNUSUAL TIMES

To support starting on time, I highly suggest that you begin the meeting at an unusual time, such as 2:17. I am not kidding. The speed limit on the Sony Pictures lot is 7 miles per hour. The speed limit at the Myrtle Beach airport is 17 miles per hour. Do you think they did a study to determine those ideal numbers? No, those numbers are weird and different, which gets people's attention.

The strange number will remain in people's awareness for days, and it will force them to mentally calculate how long it will take them to get from where they are to the meeting location in order to arrive at 2:17. You will probably get a few phone calls or e-mails asking you why the odd time. Just answer, "It's very important."

OUTLOOK SABOTAGE AND TRAVEL TIME

A complaint I hear often in my trainings is that because Microsoft Outlook (or whatever software is being used to schedule) defaults to an hour, the end time of one meeting is also the start time of another, which makes it impossible to start on time with everyone there. You must always allow for people's travel time to the meeting, and starting at odd times helps account for this, such as 10:13.

VIRTUAL MEETINGS

With virtual meetings, I suggest not only having an odd start time but also publishing an arrival time. So in the e-mail you send out, you would say, "Log in by 3:56. We start exactly at 4:02." I find it absurd that people try to log in right at the start time. Then they're late because they can't find the link or they run into connectivity problems. That's ridiculous. In the physical world, the equivalent of logging in is walking from your desk to the meeting room and possibly taking an elevator along the way, both of which should be done *before* the meeting starts, so allow for extra time. I find it comical to imagine a face-to-face meeting where everyone tries to run into the room at the exact starting time. They would all get stuck in the doorframe. Specifying an arrival time for a face-to-face meeting is also a good idea.

Everyone has too much to do and only so many minutes in a day and only so many days in a lifetime. We must respect the precious resource of time.

Having a clear agenda and respecting time lays the foundation of success for the goal of focus during the meeting. The more prepared and focused you are, the more effective and efficient the meeting will be.

GREAT MOMENTS IN MEETINGS

The Great Clock Countdown

People always used to come late, so we would lose time by starting late or by catching up the two or three chronic latecomers. We decided on a new rule. The start time would be exactly at the top of the hour based only on the clock in the conference room and no other. Once the clock was at 10 seconds before the start time, everyone would do a verbal countdown, 10, 9, 8, 7, 6, 5, 4, 3, 2, 1, and then we would start. And there was absolutely **no** catching up the latecomers. It was amazing how quickly people started coming on time.

—*Chief MD, Pathology and laboratory medicine*

GREAT MOMENTS IN MEETINGS

Stand Up and Lock the Door

The CEO of the company was ex-Air Force Academy. To keep meetings short and to the point, he would hold stand-up meetings—no chairs. He would also start exactly on time with no exceptions, at which point he would lock the door. One time a senior VP stood locked outside during the whole meeting. It didn't take long for the whole company to get the message.

—HR director, Manufacturing company

SUMMARY

1. Break the cycle.

2. Get everyone's commitment to time.

3. Start at unusual times.

4. Don't catch up the latecomers.

5. Allow for travel time.

6. Specify a log-in time for virtual meetings and an arrival time for face-to-face meetings.

PART III

DURING *and* AFTER *the* MEETING

6

Meet the Flight Crew: The Process People

When you innovate, you've got to be prepared for
people telling you that you are nuts.

—Larry Ellison

For a successful flight to occur, there are three distinct roles that must be performed by two or three process people. I call them the Pilot, the Air Traffic Controller, and the Flight Recorder. In an ideal world the Pilot, Air Traffic Controller, and Flight Recorder would be dedicated process people and not meeting participants, but I don't for a moment expect you to have that luxury. In the vast majority of meetings, the three process people will also be participants at the meeting.

Initially, people may find it distracting to play one of the process roles and be a participant. However, the roles are really simple, and like anything you learn, you first have to focus a lot of conscious attention on it, and then after a while it becomes automatic and easy. Do you remember what it was like to learn how to drive? You had to concentrate on every detail, but now you can probably drive miles and not even consciously remember the trip.

Let's meet the crew.

THE PILOT

The Pilot is the chair of the meeting and is responsible for navigating everyone successfully through the Flight Plan and agenda so that people arrive at their destination on time. Pilots are the primary timekeepers. They need to pay attention to the time allotted to each agenda item, making sure it starts and ends on time.

Within a particular agenda item, there might be some distinct subprocesses that need to be timed. For example, on a 30-minute agenda item, the new XYZ ruling, there might be a 5-minute presentation, a 5-minute question and answer, and a 20-minute discussion. Pilots need to make sure the flight stays on schedule according to the Flight Plan by monitoring the time for each process in an agenda item.

Last but not least, Pilots also make sure that participants stay within their *speaking time limit*. This is for everyone's safety and security so that the meeting doesn't get hijacked.

COMPLETING AGENDA ITEMS

When an agenda item is complete, the Pilot (or sometimes the Flight Recorder) verbally summarizes to the group what has been done or decided and what the next steps will be:

- What has been discussed

- Decisions

- Next steps

- Who will take the next steps

- When will those steps be taken

The Flight Recorder can use a copy of the agenda document to fill out this information in the last category of the Flight Plan, which is "Who is doing what and when."

THE AIR TRAFFIC CONTROLLER

The Air Traffic Controller has a huge responsibility to create focus and balance participation. In the next two chapters we will go into great detail on how this is done.

For now, to harness focus, the Air Traffic Controller will note on an erasable visual device that everyone can see the *topic* at each moment and the *process* being used (discussion, brainstorming, or something else). Then everyone knows what we are talking about and how we are talking about it.

The Air Traffic Controller is also responsible for the speaking order, giving participants clearance to speak, so that assertive people don't talk over one another and passive people don't withdraw. I call the speaking order the Queue, and from this point on, I will use Q for short. A Q can be voluntary, with people raising their hand to get in it, or the Q can be circular, in which case, you go around the room and hear from everyone.

THE FLIGHT RECORDER

The Flight Recorder's role will be critical to getting the flight into Holographic Thinking. We will go into greater detail in Chapter 9. The important point for now is that the Flight Recorder uses either a flip chart or a computer hooked up to a monitor or projector to record information during the meeting that summarizes people's points of view.

The Flight Recorder's prime responsibility is to capture people's ideas and contributions accurately. Flight Recorders do not take notes word for word. They capture with accuracy the important points people make in as few words as possible. I recommend that Flight Recorders write the same words that a speaker is using because those words are meaningful to the speaker. If Flight Recorders are not sure what to write, they may ask the speaker for clarification to make sure the recording is accurate.

It will also be the Flight Recorder's responsibility to make sure everyone receive the follow-up information they need and notes from the meeting.

THE MINUTES

If you are in the type of meeting where detailed minutes need to be kept, it is best to have a person dedicated to that function. The level of detail depends on legal requirements. Flight recording differs from minutes in the level of detail.

The function of flight recording is to create functional notes so that people can see the hologram. Too much detail in flight recording might obscure the hologram.

THE COMMITMENT KEEPER

This is an optional role that tracks actions people volunteer to take after the meeting. I have found this useful, particularly with volunteer working boards in which board members take action after a meeting. If a board meets every quarter for a two-day board meeting, it is easy to volunteer to take care of certain items and then just as easily forget about them once the meeting is over or to simply over-commit oneself.

Commitment Keepers write down any commitments people make over the course of the meeting. At the end of the meeting, they e-mail a summary of those commitments to all attendees. The Commitment Keeper should confirm the nature of the commitment with the person making the commitment at the time it is made to make sure that it is recorded accurately. It is possible for the Flight Recorder to be the Commitment Keeper and just use a separate document or flip chart page for commitments.

THE COPILOTS

This group represents everyone else in the meeting. I call them *copilots* because they too have responsibilities as keepers of the process. If the group goes off course, everyone has the right and responsibility to speak out and correct course by pointing it out. This is the only time people can speak without clearance from Air Traffic Control.

The process is not something that is inflicted upon others but rather one that everyone takes ownership of.

MERGING ROLES

In face-to-face meetings, I usually recommend having three people assume the three different roles using two different visual devices, one for the Air Traffic Controller with the topic, process, and speaking order and another for the Flight Recorder.

In a virtual meeting via computer, you share only one screen. That screen needs to be for flight recording. In virtual meetings, I have found it possible for one person to perform all three roles. The downside is that it will be harder for that individual to participate as well. Having two people is better, with Air Traffic Control essentially divided between the Pilot and the Flight Recorder.

The Pilot can watch the time and oversee the speaking order part of Air Traffic Control by keeping a list of the participants who have their virtual hand raised or calling on the next person when using a circular order. The Flight Recorder has control of the screen everyone is seeing, and is capturing the thoughts that people are sharing to create Holographic Thinking. But remember, the Air Traffic Controller also has the important responsibility to create focus on the topic and process. If the Flight Recorder uses PowerPoint, I have found that it works well to put the current topic and process in the title area of the slide and then record people's thoughts as bullets in the body of the slide.

ROTATING THE CREW

I recommend that the roles of the Pilot, Air Traffic Controller, and Flight Recorder be rotated so that everyone develops these skills in taking responsibility for the meeting. However, certain skills may predispose certain people to handling certain processes. For example, the Flight Recorder should be a person with legible handwriting if using a flip chart or good typing skills if using a computer.

Do not assume that the Pilot will be the most senior person in the organizational hierarchy. That person may want to be simply a participant, or may feel that others will be more encouraged to share their thoughts if the boss is not in charge.

In general, rotating the roles also helps distribute responsibility for the process, creates greater ownership, and prepares attendees when the usual process people cannot attend.

Process people are allowed to make necessary *process comments* without clearance from Air Traffic Control, such as the Flight Recorder's clarifying what to write to represent the speaker's point accurately. But as participants, they play by the same rules as everyone else. Pilots and Flight Recorders signal Air Traffic Controllers when they want to get in the Q, and Air Traffic Controllers put themselves in the Q if they have something to say.

GREAT MOMENTS IN MEETINGS

The Terminator

We were constantly interrupting each other during meetings, but we had one person, Joe, who excelled at it. Without directly identifying Joe, we acknowledged as a group that we had to do something about it. So we established the role of Terminator to be the person who would collect a quarter from anyone who interrupted someone else.

At the next meeting, when we all sat down, Joe pulled something out of his pocket. He slammed two rolls of quarters on the table and said, "I'm in!" We all laughed and laughed. Before we knew it, all of us—including Joe—became good at not interrupting.

—*Middle manager, Telecommunications company*

SUMMARY

Process People and Their Responsibilities

1. The Pilot

   - Navigates the agenda
   - Makes sure the meeting stays on course and on time

- Tells people how long they have to speak

- Wraps up agenda items

- Makes decisions on the fly if more time is needed for one topic and where the time will come from

2. The Air Traffic Controller

- Takes care of the visual focus device

- Keeps the topic and process boxes current and accurate

- Tracks the speaking order and gives people clearance to speak

3. The Flight Recorder

- Writes the summarized discussion points

- Notes every thought and perspective

- Sends summaries to all attendees after the meeting

4. The Commitment Keeper (may also be the Flight Recorder)

- Keeps a log of the commitments of participants and distributes them after the meeting

5. Passengers and Copilots

- Play by the rules of the Meeting Jet process

- Speak up if the meeting is going off course

7

Staying on Course
with Air Traffic Control

*To map out a course of action and follow it
to an end requires courage.*

—RALPH WALDO EMERSON

CREATING FOCUS AT THE MEETING

To bring a group of people into Holographic Thinking requires
focus. Successful focus begins in the preparation stage to make
sure each agenda item has a *purpose* and *"What do you need from
me."* Think of these two parts of each agenda item as critical lenses
that must be in place. At the meeting we will add additional lenses
to make sure that everyone is focused:

- On the same subject

- At the same time

- In the same way

- Using the same process

CREATING FOCUS WITH VISUAL DEVICES

Using visual devices is another important way to keep people focused and facilitate Holographic Thinking. A visual device is something everyone at the meeting can see. Examples are a whiteboard, flip chart, or computer connected to a monitor or projector. Some visual devices are erasable whereas others are not—that is, a whiteboard is erasable and a flip chart is not. Both erasable and nonerasable visual devices have their place in the Meeting Jet process.

For the purpose of maintaining everyone's focus on the same topic, at the same time, with the same process, an erasable visual device is best. On your erasable visual device, create a topic box and a process box. Maintaining the group's focus on the topic and process is the responsibility of the Air Traffic Controller.

In virtual meetings, it is important to make sure that everyone understands the importance of being able to see a screen and not just call in using audio. If they can't see the screen, you can assume that they are not completely focused, could be multitasking, or are in an inopportune environment to fully participate. (We will cover all this in detail in Chapter 12 on virtual meetings.)

The Topic Box

In a face-to-face meeting, I find a whiteboard useful for creating a focus on the topic and process. I draw a topic box and a process box on the left side. In virtual as well as face-to-face meetings, a simple

PowerPoint slide works well too. Put the topic and process in the title area of the slide. The bullets area will be used for flight recording, which we will discuss later.

Write whatever topic is on the floor at the moment in the topic box and whatever process the group is using in the process box. When the topic changes, the Air Traffic Controller updates the topic box. Sometimes you might add a subtopic. If you are discussing the value of instituting the Meeting Jet process in your organization, then write, "The value of instituting the Meeting Jet process" in the topic box. Perhaps at a later point in the agenda, the focus of your discussion might become more specific as in, "The value of instituting the Meeting Jet process by having Dr. Brinkman train our trainers." Make sure the topic box reflects what the group should be focused on at any particular moment if the meeting is to stay on course.

The Process Box

In the process box, the Air Traffic Controller writes the process being used in relation to the topic. For example, is the group brainstorming, or are they discussing? (More on the types of processes later.) Next to each process should be a number representing the minutes the group will focus on that topic using that specific process.

Let's say an agenda item began with a 10-minute presentation about the state of meetings in the company. Then there is a 5-minute Q&A, followed by a 20-minute discussion of the value of instituting the Meeting Jet process, and then a 10-minute subtopic of analyzing the positives and negatives of having Dr. Brinkman train their trainers. Then attendees would take a 5-minute vote on a decision whether to do it.

So in the process box, over the course of 50 minutes, we would have the following: first Presentation, 10 minutes; then Q&A, 5 minutes; then Discussion, 20 minutes; then Positives (matching), then Negatives (mismatching), 10 minutes; and finally, Decision by voting, 5 minutes. Only one process is in the process box at any given time. This keeps people focused on the same process at the same time (Figures 7.1 and 7.2).

In addition to the topic and process boxes, the flight plan (agenda) that attendees should have in front of them would show them the big picture of what they are doing and how to do it with purpose and "What do you need from me."

- #1 *Agenda item*: Instituting Meeting Jet process

- *Time*: 10:03 to 10:53 a.m. (50 minutes)

- *Who*: Geoff

- *Purpose*: To consider if we can save time and get more done by implementing a departmentwide policy on how to run meetings

- *Process with times:*

  o Presentation, 10 minutes (Geoff)

  o Q&A, 5 minutes

  o Discussion, 20 minutes

  o Matching and mismatching, 5 minutes each, total 10 minutes

  o Deciding and voting, 5 minutes

- *Info*: See attached description of the Meeting Jet process.

- *What do you need from me*: Think big (globally) about what this would mean to your team and whether it will be worth the investment of time.

- *Who is doing what and when*:

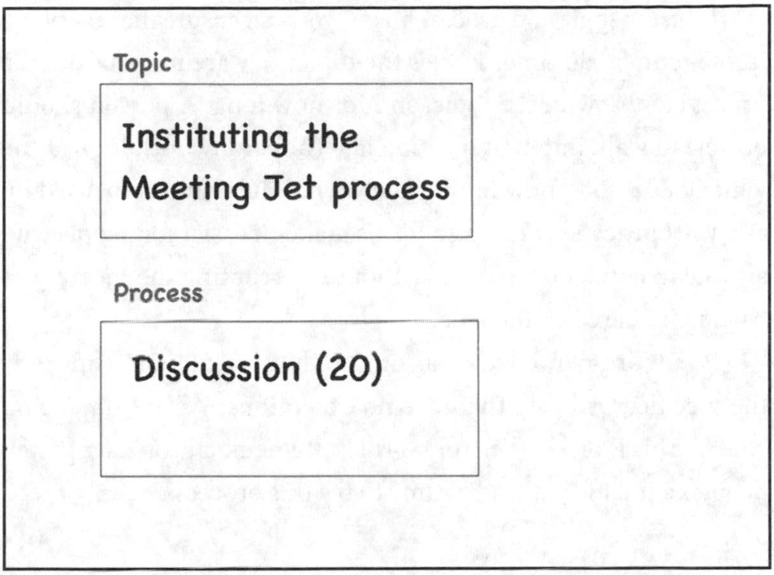

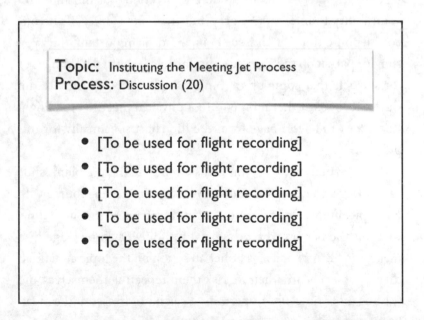

FIGURE 7.1 Air Traffic Control Topic and Process Boxes on a Whiteboard

FIGURE 7.2 Air Traffic Control Topic and Process Boxes on a PowerPoint
Slide for Virtual Meetings (or Face-to-Face)

By using topic and process boxes, you can ensure that everyone in the room at all times knows the topic they are to focus on, the process to use with the topic, and for how long. A person should be able to walk into that meeting late (hopefully not), look at the whiteboard, and know immediately what the group is focused on and what process is being used. This makes it easier for people who are late to come up to speed without interrupting the meeting to have someone catch them up.

People are allowed to speak only to the current topic using only the specified process. There are no exceptions. We are staying on course. This is one of the ground rules. Remember, you have gotten people's agreement ahead of time to try this process.

The Tarmac

If someone does veer off in a different direction, it is the Pilot's responsibility to interrupt: "Sorry, but that is off topic." If the off-course point, thought, or issue being made is important, then you should "park it on the Tarmac." The Tarmac is a visual holding area for subjects that come up that might be worthwhile but are not the topic focus at that moment. In a physical meeting, the Flight Recorder can have a page from the flip chart specifically for this purpose.

In a virtual meeting, you can switch quickly to a blank slide called Tarmac and write it down. We want to stay on course with our topic, but we don't want to forget this item. At the same time, we want the person who brought it up to feel acknowledged, so that person can refocus his or her attention on the topic at hand. If they don't feel heard, then we risk them repeating themselves and wasting more time. If time permits, it can be addressed at the meeting. If not, then it can be addressed at the next one.

EVERYONE IS A COPILOT

Keep in mind that everyone is a copilot. If the Pilot doesn't point out that the comment is off course, anyone else has the right and responsibility to do so.

Going off topic is not the only thing to watch out for. You also need to pay attention to staying in the current process. For example, if the topic is "Location of Dr. Brinkman's program" and the process is brainstorming, and someone suggests, "Our training facility" and someone else says, "That is too small," the Pilot should say immediately, "We are only brainstorming. We'll discuss considerations later. Let's continue with our process."

The purpose of the topic and process boxes is to keep everyone focused on the same thing at the same time in the same way. This keeps the meeting on course, supports Holographic Thinking, and helps you arrive at your destination on time. In the next chapter, we will experience the power of the Air Traffic Controller to balance participation.

GREAT MOMENTS IN MEETINGS

Know-It-All Pest Control

Every Wednesday we used to have a three-hour meeting. We had been doing that for years. The first time we used the Meeting Jet process, we got it done in an hour. But what really impressed us was that we got more done at higher quality. That's because we finally were able to control our Know-it-all who would take us down all these unnecessary long-winded tangents. He wasn't crazy about the process, but the rest of us loved it!

—*Quality manager, Aircraft manufacturing company*

SUMMARY

1. Use an erasable visual device to create focus on the topic and process.

2. In virtual meetings, the visual device can be a PowerPoint slide with the topic and process in the title area.

3. In face-to-face meetings, you can use a PowerPoint slide or a whiteboard.

4. There is only one topic and only one process at any given time.

5. Each process should have a number written beside it, representing the amount of time allocated for it.

6. If someone strays off course, it's the Pilot's primary responsibility to point it out and correct the course. If the Pilot does not, any participant can do so.

7. If something tangential comes up that is important, it should be parked in a separate document called the Tarmac.

8

Balancing Participation with Air Traffic Control

It's kind of fun to do the impossible.

—Walt Disney

To achieve Holographic Thinking, you need everyone's participation. The problem that usually occurs in most meetings is that the more assertive people dominate the conversation and the passive people drop out. This results in ideas being pushed through by an assertive minority opinion that does not integrate the whole.

If there is no speaking order and people just speak whenever they want to instead of listening to what the current speaker is saying, the more assertive people are concentrating on the speaker's breathing (after all, everyone must inhale at some point), waiting for the right moment to jump in and say what they have to say.

Then, if the initial speaker wasn't completely finished, he may talk over the interrupter, or he may wait for the interrupter to take a breath and then jump back in (after all, two can play at this game). Meanwhile, others in the room who didn't interrupt the original speaker quickly enough are paying even closer attention to breathing changes so that they too can have a turn.

While the assertive people play the breathing competition game, the more passive ones in the room simply drop out. Have you ever been in a meeting where you never hear from some people? For many, it is not worth it to compete to speak. The less assertive person may disagree with what is being said but chooses to remain silent. That person may have something brilliant to add, but you will never hear it. When the passive people drop out, it is like losing an eye; you no longer have depth perception. You automatically lose the hologram—and the highest value of the meeting.

At the same time, when the assertive people are competing to be heard, they are not really listening to other people's points of view. They are listening for an opening and preparing what they have to say. In a sense, you lose that eye too, and again you lose the hologram. To make matters worse, after the meeting more time will be wasted because some passive people may sabotage the agreed-upon process because they didn't really agree with it but didn't express it at the meeting. In other cases, they may feel victimized and become Whiners who make others miserable.

Whether people are being assertive or passive, without a speaking order, there isn't a lot of attention left to really listen.

THE OPPOSITE PROBLEM AT VIRTUAL MEETINGS WITH THE SAME RESULT

In a virtual meeting via computer or phone, you may run into a different problem. People can often be too polite, and when they finally do speak, they may bump into one another, making everyone a little more reserved. People may be paying attention, but you are not getting the brilliance of everyone's unique points of view, thus no hologram.

There is absolutely no point in having a meeting if you are not going to listen to and understand each other. Meetings are for sharing ideas and points of view, not for competition or hearing yourself talk. Holographic Thinking requires everyone's participation and attention.

Once you have a speaking order, there is no competition to be heard. This frees the assertive people to really listen to one another, and it allows the more passive people to feel safe enough to be heard. As each participant speaks, the others give the speaker their full attention. People feel like they are really being heard—because they are. The hologram is created, and the meeting results in higher-quality ideas.

USING AIR TRAFFIC CONTROL TO ELIMINATE REPETITION

Have you ever heard people repeat themselves at a meeting? Have you ever heard people repeat themselves at a meeting? Have you ever heard people repeat themselves at a meeting? When people repeat themselves, it usually means they have something important to say but they're not sure others have heard them. When you balance participation with a speaking order, people relax and genuinely listen. People feel heard the first time, and it eliminates repetition.

THE TWO WAYS OF USING AIR TRAFFIC CONTROL

As mentioned in Chapter 6, I refer to the speaking order as the Q (for *queue*). Air Traffic Controllers make sure that the topic and process boxes accurately reflect the focus of the meeting at all times so that someone can walk into the room and know exactly what the group is focused on and how they are focusing on it.

The Q can be utilized in three ways:

1. Voluntary—that is, raising a finger or a "virtual hand" to get in the Q

2. Preestablished circular order

3. Random order that will include everyone

Which one you use depends on other factors, such as whether the meeting is virtual or face-to-face, how many people are in the meeting, and if a group is exceptionally passive or aggressive.

Let's first discuss the voluntary Q in a face-to-face meeting. If you are using a whiteboard for Air Traffic Control, then to the right of the topic and process boxes, create some vertical space to keep a Q. The Q is a list of who is going to speak. The only way to speak at the meeting is to get in the Q.

SPECIFYING A LIMITED TIME FRAME FOR SPEAKING

To allow everyone's participation and to get the meeting done on time, there must always be a limited time frame to speak for any turn in the Q. Let's say you are going to use the process of discussion for a total of 30 minutes. The Pilot begins the discussion by reiterating the topic and process and then stating how much time each person has to speak in the Q. This is very important. If you have six people in the room for this 30-minute discussion, divide the total time by the number of people. That would mean 5 minutes per person.

However, in a discussion there needs to be some amount of back-and forth, so people may need to speak more than once. In this case, the Pilot states that there is a 2-minute time limit to speak for any one turn in the Q. Just as there is always an overall time frame for each process (that is, 30-minute discussion), there is always a limited time frame for each turn in the Q. In my experience I've have found that 2 minutes is plenty of time for people to express a point of view.

Obviously, it is critical that the total time allotted on the agenda for the discussion on this particular topic be realistic to begin with. After stating the topic, the process, and the time to speak, the Pilot asks who has something to say. A number of people will raise their finger. The Air Traffic Controller who is taking care of the whiteboard lists their names in the Q (Figure 8.1). Once people have spoken, their names are erased.

The only thing people have to do to get in the Q is raise a finger. I have found even the most passive person is willing to raise a finger, especially when the more assertive people aren't dominating. Air Traffic Controllers, who are also participants at meetings, just add themselves to the Q when they have something to say.

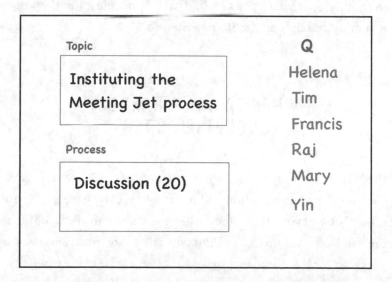

FIGURE 8.1 Air Traffic Control Topic and Process Boxes on PowerPoint with Flight Recording

WHEN TO USE A CIRCULAR Q INSTEAD OF A VOLUNTEER Q

If the meeting is virtual, it's better to use a predetermined Q even if you are using meeting software that allows attendees to raise a virtual hand. Establish an order at the beginning of the meeting—that is, alphabetical by first name or last name.

If you are on a conference call, the speaking order should definitely be predetermined and already on the agenda.

In a face-to-face meeting, a circular order is also wise because it ensures that you hear from everyone. A circular order is simple, easy, and organized. However, if there is a large number of people in the room, for the sake of time, you may need to use voluntary.

In a virtual meeting that has too many participants to utilize a circular order, the Air Traffic Controller pays attention to the "hand-raised" signal in the virtual software's control panel. In between the speakers, the Air Traffic Controller should announce the current upcoming order as in, "OK, thanks, Jack. Next we have Mary, then Sue, Marie, and Geoff." That way people know their turn is coming and they are free to pay attention.

WHEN TO USE A RANDOM SURPRISE ORDER

In a virtual meeting, if you want to make sure people are staying on their toes, paying attention, and not multitasking, have a surprise order. Let everyone know they will get a chance to speak but that the Air Traffic Controller or Pilot will call on them at random. Let people know this ahead of time and ask them to be ready when they are given clearance to speak.

ASKING QUESTIONS OF ANOTHER PARTICIPANT

I am often asked, "What if you have a question about what someone else has said?" I have experimented with ways to handle that, and I have found the simplest solution is to get in the Q to ask your question. Yes, you may be five people down, but because everyone has been relaxed and listening to each other, and because of flight recording (Chapter 9), it makes it easy to come back to what someone said previously.

If the current person in the Q has a question to clarify what someone else has said, the person being asked temporarily has the floor to answer the question—but only to answer the question. The Pilot needs to pay close attention so that the speaker doesn't expound, expand, or restate what he or she previously said. It is really the questioner's time in the Q, not that of the person answering. If the people answering questions go too far, the Pilot must cut them off gently. The Pilot should then give questioners their full two minutes in the Q if they have a point of view to express, based on the answer. In some cases, the answer to the question will suffice.

HEAD WINDS, ADDING TIME FOR AN AGENDA ITEM

Sometimes the pilot may have to make judgments on the fly, changing the amount of time dedicated to certain agenda items. For example, let's say a very fruitful discussion on a very important issue is taking place and time is running out for that item. The Pilot can make the judgment call that the discussion is more important than some other items on the agenda. As you recall from Chapter 4, "The Art of the Agenda," ordering the more important items first facilitates this kind of flexibility.

Pilots can decrease the amount of time for another item and add that time to the current discussion, or they can choose to delete an upcoming item altogether, freeing up that time. Once Pilots decide a change must be made, they should inform everyone, but in a way that doesn't disrupt the discussion. The Pilot should wait until the current person in the Q is finished speaking and then say, "Excuse me for interrupting, but I think we need a bit more time for this discussion, so we are going to put off talking about the XYZ project until next time, which gives us an additional 20 minutes for this discussion."

Then the Pilot yields the floor to the next person in the Q. However, if someone has a comment related to this process decision, he raises his hand at this moment, and the Pilot acknowledges him: "Tim, you have a thought on this decision?" And Tim might say, "Yes, I need to give the XYZ client our decision by the end of the day, and I really need an opinion from the group related to the agenda item we are postponing." In such a case, the Pilot might keep that agenda item and remove another item. Or perhaps the Pilot can suggest another option for accomplishing that result. "Why don't you, Frank, and Sally get together for 15 minutes after we are done, since you are really the major decision makers on this? Anyone else who has something to contribute can also stay."

ENDING A DISCUSSION

Another part of the Pilot's responsibility is to pay attention to the length of the Q and what it represents in future time. For example, let's say a discussion is taking place and there is only 15 minutes left on the agenda for the item. The Pilot sees that there are seven people in the Q, and a maximum of 2 minutes has been established for each turn in the Q.

If all seven people take their full 2 minutes, it will require 14 minutes. Therefore, after whoever is currently speaking is through but before the next person in the Q begins, the Pilot should say, "Excuse me for interrupting, but I see we are going to complete our time with the people remaining, so we are closing the Q." On a whiteboard the Air Traffic Controller then draws a line underneath the last person's name in the Q, and no one else is allowed in the Q unless the Pilot changes the amount of time allotted for that agenda item.

By using an Air Traffic Control Q, everyone will relax and listen to one another. Combining that with the topic and process boxes becomes exponentially more powerful. Suddenly the group is focused on the same topic, everyone is using the same process, participation is balanced, you know the timing of the flight plan (this meeting won't go on forever), and contributing is as easy as raising a finger. The Air Traffic Control Q is essential to people understanding one another's points of view, to supporting Holographic Thinking, and to producing higher-quality integrated ideas and results.

THE AUDITORY SIGNAL FOR AGREEMENT

An important part of the Meeting Jet process for face-to-face meetings will be for the group to establish an auditory signal that represents "agreement" but doesn't drown out the speaker. This signal cannot be used in virtual meetings or conference calls, but it is very effective in face-to-face meetings. Here are some examples: rapping on the table (which is what the Canadian Parliament does), tapping a pen on a glass, doing the golf clap (a quiet clap), or saying "Hear, hear."

This is an important part of the process for a number of reasons. Imagine the group is in a discussion and there are seven people in the Q who have a maximum of two minutes each. If Mary is the seventh person and she wants us to know where she stands on what some of the other people before her said, she might spend her entire two minutes reiterating what they had said to note her agreement. Perhaps she actually has something else to contribute with her two minutes, but she will use up her time reiterating. Even if people have nothing new to contribute to the discussion but want to let the group know where they stand, they will have to get in the Q. An auditory signal saves time. People don't need to get in the Q just to let others know they agree.

When using the auditory signal, often the last few people in a Q will drop themselves off the list because they have already let the group know where they stand. Or if they feel the need to reinforce something that has been said, they usually add another dimension to it, which tends to shorten discussion time while increasing its quality.

The auditory signal also speeds things up by taking the group's temperature on a point of view rather quickly. If Mark says, "I think we should survey the membership to find out what they think the priorities of the national association should be," and suddenly 10 of 10 people are tapping their glass, then you immediately know how important that point is to the group.

Another advantage of the auditory signal is to give speakers some sort of feedback. Owing to the orderliness of the Q and the polite listening atmosphere that occurs when using the Meeting Jet process, speakers are addressing a quiet room. The auditory signal serves as an acknowledgment to speakers of their contribution.

Take note, there is no signal for disagreement. If you have a consideration or differing point of view, you will just get in the Q and state it when it's your turn.

Criteria for the Auditory Signal

Everyone in the room will be using the same signal, so it is important that the group agree what that signal will be ahead of time. This shouldn't take more than five minutes. Write the criteria for the auditory signal on a flip chart and then have the group make some suggestions that fulfill all of the criteria. Then have them vote. Done.

The criteria for establishing your signal are as follows:

1. It must be auditory.

2. It must not be so loud that it distracts from what the speaker is saying.

3. Everyone must be willing and able to do it.

I have sat in on meetings in which the group has implemented my Meeting Jet process but left out the auditory signal. It is not the same. Trust me on this; you need to try it to experience its usefulness. Encourage everyone to use it. It will make a big difference, in terms of saving time, decreasing repetition, giving speakers the feeling that they were heard, taking the group's temperature on an idea quickly, and uplifting the energy of the meeting.

Auditory Signals for Virtual Meetings and Conference Calls

It is completely out of the question to use the auditory signal on conference calls or in virtual meetings because it would get in the way of hearing the speaker. However, when using virtual meeting software, if you have everyone's webcams turned on, it is possible to have a visual signal, such as a thumbs-up or silent clapping, which will accomplish the same purpose.

In the next chapter we'll explore another critical factor in creating the hologram: flight recording.

GREAT MOMENTS IN MEETINGS

The One That Almost Got Away

At a strategic planning conference that I facilitated, we broke into four groups of 20 people each. Each group had a computer projecting onto a screen on which to take notes on what people said. The participants in each group sat around in a circle. I instructed the facilitator of each group to use a circular Q to hear from everyone as many times as the period for each agenda item allowed.

Afterward, a woman in my group told me that in a group like this she never would have volunteered to speak. But because it was so relaxed and everyone had a turn, she felt comfortable contributing. In my opinion, what she contributed each time she spoke was brilliant. Had we not used the circular Q, we never would have heard from her, and her brilliance would have been lost.

—*Dr. Rick Brinkman*

I Grunt You

When I joined a particular board that had a history of dysfunction and infighting, I suggested that the auditory signal be grunting. That's right, grunting. I chose grunting because it was fun to do and it lightened everyone up. Even though some were reluctant and embarrassed at first, most people began to enjoy grunting, although others reserved the right to just say the words, "grunt, grunt." That was close enough.

Our meetings transformed. As years passed, people used the word "grunt" in an additional way. They would say to each other, "I grunt what you are saying." As new members joined the board, they all started using "grunt" in the same way without its ever being explained to them!

—*Dr. Rick Brinkman*

SUMMARY

1. Air Traffic Control is about creating a speaking order called a Q.

2. If there is no official speaking order, then

   - The assertive people compete to speak, interrupting one another and not really listening to one another.

   - The passive people drop out and remain silent.

3. The Q can be utilized in the following three ways:

   - Voluntary: raising a finger or a "virtual hand"

   - Preestablished circular order

   - Random order that includes everyone

4. There must always be a time limit to speak for any turn in the Q.

5. In virtual meetings and conference calls, a circular order should be used.

6. The Pilot may add time to a process from another topic of lower priority.

7. The Pilot must close the Q at some point to keep the meeting on course and on time.

8. An auditory signal should be established for face-to-face meetings.

- Criteria for the signal

  o It must be auditory.

  o It must not be so loud that it distracts from what the speaker is saying.

  o Everyone must be willing and able to do it.

- There is no auditory signal for conference calls or virtual meetings. You can use a visual signal instead.

9

Visual Flight Recording: Don't Let a Good Idea Get Away

We are visual creatures. When you doodle an image that captures the essence of an idea, you not only remember it but you also help other people understand and act on it—which is generally the point of meetings in the first place.

—Tom Wujec

The other visual device that you should use at your meetings is for flight recording. Its purpose is to make sure you do not let a good idea get away. Using visual recording will exponentially enhance people's ability to see the hologram and make it easy to follow up with actions based on the meeting.

THE TWO SUPERPOWERS OF VISUAL COMMUNICATION

Let's examine the differences between auditory (verbal) communication that you hear and visual communication that you see. Visual communication has two superpowers that auditory communication does not have:

1. It remains over time.

2. You can see a totality of concepts.

I worked with an ex-couple who were fighting over their kid. I met with each separately for an hour and then brought them together. I began by saying, "I must say I am most impressed with how much you both agree with each other." It was funny to watch their reactions, as they both folded their arms, crossed their legs, leaned back, and looked at me as if I were crazy.

I continued, "Correct me if I'm wrong. Do either of you want your child to be traumatized? I didn't think so. Do either of you want your child to develop emotional problems? I didn't think so. Do either of you want your child to learn your communication behavior so he can experience it someday with his spouse? I didn't think so."

I then walked over to the whiteboard and said, "So it's my understanding that we are here in the best interests of David." And I wrote in big letters, "Best Interests of David." And for the first time in a year, they weren't adversaries but suddenly allies with a very important common purpose. I strategically wrote that on the whiteboard because I wanted that concept to be visual so it would stay in their awareness throughout the visit.

Always remember that people can pay attention to only seven, give or take two, things consciously at one time. By making something visual, it is easier to keep it in awareness because it remains over time. "Best Interests of David" was with us at that moment, 5 minutes later, 20 minutes later, and through the end of the visit. Auditory communication exists only the moment you say it and then it's gone! So visual superpower 1 is the ability to remain over time.

The second power visual communication has is that it enables you to see a totality of concepts. If we were discussing where to eat, we might consider the criteria we need to satisfy. So we might write the following:

- In and out within an hour

- On the way home

- Won't cost too much

- Nice quiet place where we can relax

You can't say or hear all of those at the same time, but if we make them visual, it's easier to see the totality of all the factors we want to satisfy.

If a meeting is run strictly with auditory communication and no visuals and I have a thought that I feel is important to the group mind, I am going to repeat it a number of times as a way of keeping it in people's awareness. Others who agree with my thought may also repeat it to emphasize it. However, the people who don't agree and who have a different perspective will repeat theirs a number of times to keep it in everyone's awareness. Suddenly we have dueling banjos of repetitive thoughts at this meeting. It's a common occurrence I have observed in over 30 years of studying human behavior. Whenever people do not feel heard and understood, they will repeat themselves. When people repeat themselves, they really need feedback, some sort of acknowledgment that you understand what they are trying to say.

However, if my thought is made visual, it is an acknowledgment that I have been heard and my contribution is treasured enough to be carved in digital stone or written on a flip chart. Even better, I not only see it, I see that you see it too, and that visual remains for the duration of the meeting, which deepens the feeling of being heard. Visual flight recording will wipe out the majority of repetitions at a meeting and save you lots of time.

It also supports the collective understanding of all the factors in the discussion. Each point that people make is another piece of the holographic puzzle. As we contribute our individual pieces, the group rises into Holographic Thinking. Participants will feel that they are part of a greater whole.

By visually recording, you are also taking high-quality notes that facilitate effective follow-up. Adding visual recording to a good meeting takes it to a higher level.

The Visual Flight Recording Device

This visual device, unlike the one used for our topic and process boxes, does not need to be erasable. It can be a flip chart or a computer attached to a projector, but it must be clearly visible to the whole group. I have found a blank PowerPoint slide to be great for flight recording in both face-to-face and virtual meetings. A whiteboard is not a good idea because when it is full, you must erase it. Obviously you can take a picture of the whiteboard. But then that data will have to be rewritten in digital form to send to everyone after the meeting. The same is true for a flip chart, as it too will need to be rewritten for proper follow-up.

On the other hand, when using PowerPoint, the disadvantage is that once the current slide is full, it must be replaced with another slide. For the purpose of seeing the hologram, having everyone see all the points related to a discussion at the same time is highly desirable. In that case, in a face-to-face meeting, it may be more desirable to flight record on a flip chart. When a page is full, you can stick it on the wall, thereby seeing the totality of points on multiple pages all at once.

When using a PowerPoint slide, I shrink the font as we go along to fit more points on one slide, but you can take that only so far. Once you are below 18 points, you usually will need to start another slide.

I once led a virtual strategic planning meeting that included close to 50 participants. Our discussions were long and required multiple slides of notes. To help people see the big picture, every so often, I would go back a few slides and do a review for the group by showing the slides and reading the points out loud. It worked quite well.

Your choice of visual devices often comes down to logistics and/or the nature of the agenda item. First, is the meeting virtual or face-to-face? Second, if face-to-face, is the discussion complex and lengthy enough that it is important to see all factors at once? And third, factor in the importance of efficiency by having the discussion already in digital form versus transcribing it later.

Combining Flight Recording with Air Traffic Control

Sometimes I am asked if the topic box, process box, Q, and flight recording can be combined in one place. That depends. On a Power-Point slide, I recommend putting the topic and process in the title area of the slide and using bullet points for flight recording, thereby combining the Air Traffic Control aspect of focus on topic and process. In a virtual meeting the Q should be a predetermined circular order written on the agenda. The Pilot will call on people to speak on the basis of that predetermined order. So in that case the Flight Recorder is doing part of Air Traffic Control (topic and process) while the Pilot is doing the Q. In this scenario there is no separate Air Traffic Controller needed.

If we are using a voluntary Q as in a face-to-face meeting, I prefer to have the Q on a whiteboard. Once you have the whiteboard, you might as well also use it for topic and process, if only to give you more room on the PowerPoint slide for flight recording. In this case the Air Traffic Controller is responsible for the topic box, the process box, and the Q on the whiteboard, and the Flight Recorder is responsible for capturing people's ideas on a projected computer or flip chart.

Making Sure the Flight Recording Is Accurate

Let's say Ian is the Flight Recorder (at a flip chart or computer) and Jane, the first person in the Q, speaks. Ian then summarizes Jane's point of view in one or two sentences, as briefly as possible while still capturing the essence. Since Jane can see what Ian is writing, she can make sure that Ian accurately represents her point of view. If Ian is accurately portraying Jane's point, then Jane says nothing and the Q continues to the next person. If there is a discrepancy or if Jane feels there is more that needs to be added, she simply says so, and Ian corrects it or adds it. If Ian is not clear about how to summarize Jane's point of view, he simply asks Jane what should be written.

This is the value of everyone being able to see what is being recorded. If Ian were taking notes on a laptop computer and Jane couldn't see what was being written, it would be all too easy for Ian to misinterpret what Jane was saying or to leave out important points she was making.

AFTER THE MEETING: FOLLOW-UP

The goal of the meeting is to accomplish something of value, so effective follow-up after a meeting is vital.

It will be the Flight Recorder's responsibility to make sure everyone receives the follow-up information he or she needs from the meeting. If notes were handwritten on a flip chart, those notes need to be transcribed in electronic format. If the flight recordings of all the discussions, brainstorms, and so on were taken on a computer, a big step has already been accomplished.

Everyone at the meeting should receive a complete copy of the flight recording. Those who were given the option of not attending the meeting but were promised notes should also receive it. Make sure the subject line of the e-mail is clear—that is, "Complete Notes: Staff Meeting, Monday, June 5, 2016."

There may be some attendees who will be responsible for follow-up actions related to one particular agenda item. For example, let's say one item on the agenda was to "look into how the move would affect the morale of X department." Those responsible for following up on that should receive a separate e-mail with any notes pertaining to that particular item—for example, "Notes Related to Morale Implications, Staff Meeting, Monday, June 5, 2016."

Although these notes were contained within the complete flight recording document, I recommend that individuals receive separate notes related to items they need to take action on. This will serve as a reminder, as well as an easy reference to the information they need related to those actions.

Effective follow-up also requires accountability, which can depend on how an organization or team tracks its projects. I have met people who have group whiteboards, project tracking software, or some other means. In terms of meetings, part of a team meeting can be used to go in circular order, during which time everyone reports on what they have done and where they stand on the commitments they made at the last meeting.

In the Meeting Jet process, you keep the flight on course through Air Traffic Control by focusing on the same thing at the same time with the topic and process boxes. You eliminate competition to speak with the Air Traffic Control Q, so that everyone relaxes, participates, and truly listens to the others. With flight recording, you acknowledge people's contributions as well as see the totality of factors with a visual summary. And like magic, before you know it, everyone is in Holographic Thinking. As a bonus, you have terrific notes ready for effective follow-up action.

GREAT MOMENTS IN MEETINGS

Teenage, Mutant, Anal Engineers

At an engineering firm where I once worked, we had a companywide meeting process. There was always an agenda, and we would stick to it. The agenda made it clear what result was expected by meeting's end.

When you came in, there was a basket for cell phones, and all laptops had to be shut down. The only exception was the laptop for the notetaker. Action items and takeaways were always written on the whiteboard, and if you were late, there was no catch-up.

If items came up that were off topic, they were put on a flip chart we called the Parking Lot, and at the end of the meeting, it was decided what would be done with each of those items.

They were a bunch of anal engineers, but the process sure worked.

—*HR director, Engineering firm*

SUMMARY

1. The two superpowers of visual recording are these:

- Persists over time

- Lets you see the totality of concepts

2. Side effects

- People feel their contributions are acknowledged

- Reduces repetition

3. Decide which device to use

- Virtual

  o Shared screen

- Face-to-face

  o Flip chart if discussion is complex because all points need to be seen at the same time

  o Projected computer screen

4. Flight Recorder responsibilities

- Check accuracy of notes.

- Follow up.

  o E-mail people the complete notes.

  o Send separate notes on specific items to those responsible for follow-up actions.

10

In-Flight Entertainment: Criteria

*If there is any one secret of success, it lies in the ability to
get the other person's point of view and see things from
that person's angle as well as from your own.*

—HENRY FORD

Now that we have the crew's roles and the safety demo of how to run a meeting, it's time to examine some of the processes we will use in our process box. Since one of the primary goals at meetings is to make sure that everyone can see everyone else's point of view, it is very important that people communicate clearly. This requires attendees to have an understanding of intent and criteria.

Intent is purpose. Each agenda item will already have a specified purpose on the agenda. Knowing the purpose of an item is one of the lenses that focus people properly at a meeting. Another lens is *criteria*—that is, the relevant factors to satisfy. Anytime ideas are being discussed, assume you don't understand them fully if you don't yet know their intent and criteria.

I still remember the first time I became aware of criteria in communication. I was in my office with a couple. It was the end of the visit, and she suddenly turned to him and said, "Honey, let's go to the Rose Gardens."

His response was, "Nah."

She looked very disappointed, so I asked, "What's the intent behind going to the Rose Gardens? Why did you suggest that?"

She said, "We have an hour before we have to pick up the kids. We are feeling closer than we have in a long time. So I thought it would be nice to spend some quiet time together."

He then said, "That's a great idea, but it's too hot and buggy. How about the café we've been meaning to try?"

She delightedly said, "Sure!"

Now I ask you, do you think she really cared about going to the Rose Gardens? No. What she cared about was spending time together. That's the intent. The Rose Gardens were just a way to fulfill that intent. But why did she choose that? Why not dinner for two or a movie or a cruise? The answer was the criteria. They had only an hour before they had to pick up the kids, so there was a time criterion. Perhaps the Rose Gardens were on the way home, so the geographic criterion may have supported the time criterion. There might have been a budgetary criterion: the gardens wouldn't cost anything. Atmospheric criterion: it was a nice quiet place. Perhaps it was a place of meaning for them, or the opposite, a place completely new so they could experience it together. All those factors were criteria.

Criteria are the reasons people like or dislike ideas. The criteria can be positive or negative. People may reject an idea because it violates a criterion they think is important or it doesn't fulfill a criterion they value.

In studying communication for over 30 years, I have noticed that people usually do not communicate their intent or criteria. They blurt out an idea. Assume you know nothing until you know people's intent and criteria. And when you are presenting an idea, you have told people nothing until you tell them your intent and criteria.

Criteria explain why people think what they think. This helps others understand their point of view. The Flight Recorder will want to listen carefully for criteria and make sure they are written down for everyone to see, perhaps on a separate list from the ideas themselves. You may not know the relevant criteria before the discussion starts, but as it progresses, those criteria will be revealed. Listen for them and create a list. People's ideas may not be feasible, but the criteria behind them can be important.

The proper order of communication is the following:

1. Intent

2. Criteria

3. Idea

Let's say a team is discussing having a leadership training. The group is in the phase during which they are trying to decide where to hold this seminar. The subintent at this point is to "find the right facility that will allow people to get the most value out of the training." Different venues are suggested as possible locations. It is at this point that criteria become critical.

One person at the meeting says it should be in our own facility, another says we should go to a hotel, and a third insists that going away to the resort is the only way to go. We can go round and round in this meeting with people taking sides for our own conference room, the hotel, or the resort. We can even get into conflict over it if the issue is significant to everyone in the room.

But what are we really talking about? We need to ask people why they think what they think to reveal criteria. Asking the first person about doing it in our own conference room might reveal, "Well, if we do it in our own facility, then it won't cost us anything." That person is looking at a budgetary criterion.

The person pushing the hotel might respond to the same question with, "I am concerned that if we do it in our own facility, people will run and get their messages and be distracted. If we are going to invest the time and money, we really should focus." This person's highly valued criterion is focus.

The third person, who supports the idea of the resort, might respond by saying, "I think if we are going to do it, we should get away together for a few days. Then we are going to bond together as a team." The highly valued criteria for this person are bonding and teamwork.

We are really not all talking about the same thing here. One person is talking about the budget, the next focus, and the third teamwork. But until we expose the criteria consciously, we could be under the illusion that we are talking about the same thing and even get into conflict over it.

STATE YOUR CRITERIA AND DETERMINE THE CRITERIA OF OTHERS

At meetings, it is imperative that everyone understand the importance of criteria so that they can communicate clearly why they think what they think and also so they can clarify others' unexpressed criteria. People's ideas are usually nothing more than a means to an end. And that end is the fulfillment of an overall intent and a list of criteria. Ask people to specify the criteria they are attempting to satisfy when they communicate their thoughts. Encourage them to ask for the criteria of others if these are not volunteered.

HIGHER-POWER LENS FOCUS: START WITH INTENT AND CRITERIA

Before starting a discussion, the first thing that should be done is to state the group's intent, which is what it is trying accomplish with the discussion, and then list the relevant criteria that need to be satisfied. This can save quite a bit of time.

The list of criteria should be prioritized. Some criteria may be negotiable whereas others are not. For example, a federal agency is having a leadership retreat, but they cannot use taxpayer dollars to cater it. The attendees will need to go out for lunch and pay for it themselves. Since they want to make the most out of their retreat time, their criteria for lunch might include the following:

- Time (within an hour)

- A variety of food that would satisfy all attendees

- A certain budget range

In investigating the options, they might find that having a caterer bring in lunch would definitely satisfy the time criterion. But then the caterer limits the choices to only three items and charges an additional 20 percent, which violates the criteria of variety and budget. Once they realize that catering is not an option, a couple of subcriteria are added to the list:

- Time (within an hour)

  o Geographically close

  o Quick service

- A variety of food that will satisfy all attendees

- A certain budget range

When people say what they like or don't like about an idea, it is based on their criteria. Going back to the example of the team deciding where to hold the leadership training, some of the positive criteria for holding it in their own facility might include these:

- People will have no trouble finding it.

- It will save money since we don't have to pay for the venue.

- If a person attending the meeting is needed for an emergency, he or she can be easily found.

When we hear from the attendees who don't like that idea, we find the following criteria:

- There's the risk of unnecessary distractions. Others might poke their heads in the room to see what is going on.

- People will run out and check their messages on breaks and come back late.

- So-called urgencies will come up, and people will be pulled out of the room even though the problems could have easily been handled by others and probably would have been handled if the meeting participants weren't so readily available.

RECOGNIZE THAT PEOPLE PLAY A CRITERIA ROLE

Over time you may learn that some participants at your meetings tend to focus on particular criteria. For example, one person may always be paying attention to the budget, whereas someone else is always tuned into morale implications.

Once you know this, those people become resources for the team. You can depend on them to pay attention in a certain way to make sure those criteria are considered.

HOW TO EXTRACT CRITERIA

The magic questions to ask to extract criteria are these: "Why do you say that?" and "What will that accomplish?" The more quickly we extract everyone's criteria, the more quickly the group will come up with the best solutions.

Here is an example. A company's executives had to break some bad news to their employees. Because of the economic downturn, employees would have to begin to contribute to their health insurance benefits. There was a concern among all managers that this would demoralize their employees. The managers all agreed on the intent: they wanted to minimize upset. However, there was some disagreement on what was the best way to do this. Some managers thought it would be best tackled in a companywide meeting, whereas others thought it should be done in many small group meetings. It started to get contentious, and management polarized into two camps.

I was presenting a full-day program at their leadership retreat, and they asked me to help them with this issue. They carved out two hours on the agenda to address this subject. I knew it wouldn't take that long, and I was right. I simply went in circular order, asking each faction what they were trying to accomplish and what they were trying to avoid, to extract their important positive and negative criteria. Here's what they said:

Supporters of the Large Group Format: Positive Criteria

- "Everyone will hear the same communication at the same time in exactly the same way."

Supporters of the Large Group Format: Negative Criteria

- "If it is done in small groups, it will take days to do it. The rumor mill will go wild, and people will be hearing it second- and third-hand, with exaggeration and misinformation."

- "If the presentation is given by management 16 times to cover all the groups, it will no longer be the same presentation. People will not be hearing the same thing."

Supporters of the Small Group Format: Positive Criteria

- "People will immediately have questions about their benefits and how it will affect them financially. In a small group, managers can share specific information with each employee immediately."

Supporters of the Small Group Format: Negative Criteria

- "You will drop this news on people, but then it will take a number of days to inform individuals how it will affect each of them financially, so they will be worrying for days."

Putting it all together, the positive criteria for both large and small group supporters were as follows:

- "We want people to hear the same communication at the same time in exactly the same way."

- "We want to answer their questions immediately about their benefits and how this change will affect them personally."

Putting it all together, the negative criteria of what they wanted to avoid for both large and small group supporters were as follows:

- Taking days to do it and having people spend those days worrying

- Having employees hear the message through the rumor mill and be misinformed

- Having the formal presentation evolve and change by doing it multiple times

Once all the positive and negative criteria were made visual by the Flight Recorder, the group arrived at Holographic Thinking, and the answer became obvious to everyone in the room. They would inform people in one large group so that everyone would hear the same thing at the same time in the same way from the senior leadership. Then they would immediately divide up into smaller groups with people assigned to facilitators who would have their personal information and could answer all their financial questions.

It took only 20 minutes to arrive at this unanimous decision by the group. By using the Meeting Jet process and exposing all the positive and negative criteria, the managers were able to have the blinding flash of the obvious that gave them all the positives while minimizing the negatives.

But had they begun their initial discussions by first listing the positive criteria they wanted to satisfy and the negative criteria they wanted to avoid, they would have arrived at a solution much more efficiently.

The Mutual Aid Agreement

In the early 1990s, I was the facilitator of a meeting organized by the Marin County Fire Chiefs Association. We were meeting to update the mutual aid agreement between the 22 different fire departments in the county. Prior to that, the agreement was informal and not in writing. There were also varying interpretations of that agreement.

We chose a place that was comfortable, allowing for a work environment that was informal, with whiteboards and plenty of wall space to post flip charts. It was neutral and had the appropriate conveniences. We wanted to create a spirit of collaboration and appreciation, that we were getting together to help each other out, for the greater good of the fire safety of the county.

As a facilitator, I've found that concepts unite and details divide. The trick is to make sure people feel comfortable enough to express their differences openly. The issues must be depersonalized.

So whenever we arrived at a point of disagreement, I made sure everyone had a chance to speak, and I summarized on the flip chart what that person said. One of the ground rules was that people had to be honest about what they thought. With each issue, we would list first all the pros and then all the cons.

By having everyone see the chart and look at all the factors, it depersonalized the discussion. In addition, it got people to see a bigger picture than the one they had before the meeting.

That led to a simple philosophical agreement on mutual aid, which is in effect to this day, is evolving as times change, and is getting better every year.

—*Fire chief, Volunteer facilitator*

SUMMARY

As a Group

1. Begin discussions by stating the intent and making a list of relevant criteria.

2. As discussions progress and other criteria surface, add them to the criteria list, which you keep visible to everyone.

3. If you don't know the criteria before a discussion starts, create the criteria list on the basis of what people say during the discussion.

As an Individual

1. Begin by stating your intent.

2. When presenting an idea, outline your thinking and the significant criteria (reasons) for your recommendations.

3. Always offer the group a number of options. Specify the positive criteria and negative criteria of each option and then give your recommendation. In your presentation you may want to state the reasons you have rejected certain options so people understand your thinking.

4. When people are sharing their ideas and opinions, assume you don't fully understand until you know their intent and criteria. Take responsibility to clarify those by asking questions.

11

In-Flight Entertainment: Meeting Processes

*Those who say it cannot be done
should not interrupt those doing it.*

—CHINESE PROVERB

There are eight different processes that you can use at a meeting. All are not used at every meeting. Which processes are used simply depends on what you are trying to accomplish with each agenda item. However, some processes usually go together or in sequence.

Let's explore the eight meeting processes:

1. Brainstorming

2. Matching

3. Mismatching

4. Discussion

5. Presentation

6. Question and answer (Q&A)

7. Rating, voting, and decision-making

8. Follow-up

As we have explored, to create focus at a meeting everyone must be focused on the same topic and use the same process. This is why we have the topic and process boxes on an erasable visual device. Only one process can be performed at a time, so there should always be only one process in our Air Traffic Control process box. The only exception to this rule is presentation and Q&A, which we will explore shortly. In addition, all processes must have a time frame, which is also written in the process box.

There are typically five processes used for generating and analyzing ideas: brainstorming, matching, mismatching, rating, and discussion.

BRAINSTORMING

In a brainstorm, participants volunteer ideas without any qualification, restriction, or comment by others. Participants are encouraged to think aloud and suggest as many ideas as possible, no matter how outlandish or bizarre. The intent is to generate creative ideas and solutions. After the brainstorm, the ideas go through an analysis that includes extracting the participants' criteria.

In one of my seminars, we did an exercise to generate outrageous customer service ideas for a healthcare professional's office. One person said, "I want a hot tub in the waiting room."

To extract the criteria, we asked, "Why? What would that do for you?"

He said, "Then I would be relaxing instead of waiting."

Another person in the group volunteered, "My chiropractor has a relaxation room with soft lighting, comfortable lounge chairs, and soft relaxing music with nature sounds. I'm disappointed when he comes to get me."

Behind every outrageous idea there are valuable criteria that may be fulfilled in a different way. Always dig a little deeper to uncover them.

MATCHING AND MISMATCHING

Matching is when participants state only what they like about the current idea. *Mismatching* is when participants state only what they don't like about the current idea. You do both to analyze a particular idea, but they must always be done separately. I can't emphasize this enough. By separating the two, you get the group to step back in a neutral fashion from any preformed opinions they may have. As a team, the group first collects all matches for an idea, and once that process is complete, they switch to mismatch. If you go in circular order and let people say either a match or a mismatch, they will express only that which fits their opinion. In an unstructured meeting, simultaneous match and mismatch is what tends to happen. When people say something they like about an idea, others respond with, "Yeah, but . . ."

In general, I suggest doing matching first. Once you identify everything that you like about an idea, it puts the mismatches in a different perspective, as just criteria to address to make the idea happen.

You can flight record matching and mismatching in two ways, in columns or in an outline. When you are using a flip chart, the Flight

Recorder writes the idea at the top with a line down the middle. In one column the Flight Recorder writes all the matches, and in the other, all the mismatches. If you are using a computer connected to a monitor as your visual device, I recommend using an outlining program. Create a heading representing the idea and subheadings for matching and mismatching. Again, you never match and mismatch at the same time. This only invites a shooting gallery or a tug-of-war.

RATING

After the matching and mismatching process, it's a good idea to rate the ideas on the basis of relative priority. You could have an idea that has only three matches and eight mismatches. However, the importance of the three matches greatly outweighs the significance of the eight mismatches. In that case, the eight mismatches are considerations to work out with further thought, or perhaps they are not relevant.

Maybe it's the other way around. There are eight matches but only one mismatch that is huge such as, "Federal regulations make it illegal." In that case, you need the group to go back to the intent they are trying to accomplish, include the federal regulation on the list of criteria, and go back to brainstorming.

Once you have gone through all the matches and mismatches and prioritized them, you may switch to a discussion. Now that people see the big picture of all the positive and negative factors, you want to hear from everyone what they think.

GOING IN A CIRCLE TO STAY ON COURSE

When using the processes of brainstorming, matching, or mismatching, don't use the volunteer Q. Establish a circular order and go around the room, letting people say one idea, match, or mismatch (depending on the process being used at the time). In a typical brainstorm in which people just call things out, it can be hard for the Flight Recorder to keep up. When it is their turn in the circular order, people aren't required to offer an idea. They can pass. Continue until either the time limit established for the process is up or the group runs out of ideas to add. In virtual meetings, the circular Q is always preferable to the voluntary. In a phone-only meeting, a predetermined order is required, but a conference call is not recommended for idea analysis because the lack of visuals prevents participants from seeing all factors at once.

If the meeting has more than 20 attendees and time is limited, you may want to allow people to give voice to more than one idea when it's their turn to speak.

PRESENTATION

The *presentation* part of the process is when a person expounds on an idea, proposal, or report to the group without interruption or questions. It is good for a presenter to have visuals—that is, PowerPoint—but the presenter should never simply read off the PowerPoint. The slides should have bullets that include facts, figures, and important ideas the presenter elaborates on.

QUESTION AND ANSWER

This process usually follows a presentation, but it also can take place during the course of the presentation. The latter is the only situation in which there can be two processes in the process box.

It can save time to separate them because questions may be asked that will be answered by the presentation itself. In that case, a presenter may defer them. However, an advantage of merging them is that the presenter may leave out some underlying fact or assumption that is critical to the group's understanding, and a well-timed question will uncover that missing piece.

DISCUSSION

This is one of the most important interactions at a meeting. In a *discussion*, participants offer their opinions or points of view on a particular topic, during which additional important criteria often will be revealed. A strict time limit should be established beforehand for each turn in the Q. When determining the overall time frame for a discussion process, you will need to consider the following:

1. The nature of the topic—that is, whether it is a "hot topic," where there may be differences of opinion to be resolved, or a "fun topic," where everyone will have something to say, or a "crickets topic," where no one will want to say anything.

2. The number of attendees—consider the factors in the first consideration above multiplied by the number of people.

3. How much you think they will have to say.

4. The amount of time available—have enough time for multiple turns in the Q so that people can respond to one another.

This is where having a realistic sense of time comes in handy when creating the agenda. Otherwise, you set the group up for failure. Make sure you always make a note of how long a discussion actually takes or how much more time was necessary.

RATING, VOTING, AND DECISION-MAKING

Rating is when the group prioritizes a list of items. The items can be a list of criteria gathered during matching or mismatching or during a brainstorm or discussion.

Let's say we have a list of criteria on a flip chart, and we want to get a sense of the relative priorities of the criteria. I might ask people to copy the list on a piece of paper and rate each one on a scale of 1 to 5 with 1 being least important and 5 most important. Then I would go in circular order around the room and put people's numbers next to each of the criteria. Once we add the numbers, voilà, we have a rating of priority.

Voting involves making a decision on the agenda item discussed.

How decisions are made in an organization depends on its hierarchy and culture. Sometimes people provide their input and the one in command makes the decision, whereas in other cases, such as a board of directors, a vote determines the outcome.

FOLLOW-UP

The Flight Recorder's responsibility in follow-up is threefold. One, at the end of each agenda item, the Flight Recorder or the Pilot (if those roles are merged) should summarize the following:

- What has been discussed

- Decisions

- Next steps

- Who will take the next steps

- When they will take them

Two, the Flight Recorder should send complete notes to all participants, resource people, and need-to-know people. Three, the Flight Recorder should excerpt the actions or commitments plus related notes each individual will take. The Flight Recorder should send them in separate e-mails with clear subject lines.

GREAT MOMENTS IN MEETINGS

The Volunteer Games

I was on a board of directors where people resisted officer positions. Whenever we asked, "Who is interested?" all we heard in the room was crickets. Then the few of us who always stepped forward would step forward again. After a few years of that, those of us who always volunteered realized we needed to create a more sustainable model of leadership development.

I proposed that if we couldn't work it out, the fallback position would be to roll dice, and those who had already served in the role would not be eligible. So if you hadn't served in that role, you would receive a number from 1 to 6, and we would roll the dice for treasurer, secretary, and the other positions. In creating the agenda, I decided to inject a little humor by writing the following:

Agenda item: Officer elections

Time: 10:49 to whenever (No one leaves until it's done.)

Purpose: Decide on the president-elect, VP, secretary, and treasurer.

Process:

- Discuss.

- Nominate.

- Try to hide under the table.

- Have to suddenly run to the bathroom.

- Pretend to receive an important call.

- Go through the stages of grief.

- Accept the inevitable.

- Bite the bullet and go for it.

And you know what, it worked. We didn't have to come down to dice.

—Past president, Volunteer working board member

SUMMARY

The eight meeting processes:

1. Brainstorming

2. Matching

3. Mismatching

4. Discussion

5. Presentation

6. Question and answer (Q&A)

7. Rating, voting, and decision-making

8. Follow-up

12

Virtual Meetings and Conference Calls

I exist in two places. Here and where you are.

—Margaret Atwood

I n today's world, business meetings aren't bound by geography. Conference calls and virtual meetings are standard business practice in most organizations. When I use the term *conference call*, I'm referring to people meeting via phone, and I am assuming there is no shared screen that participants can see. When I use the term *virtual meeting*, I am referring to using meeting software—for example, GoToMeeting, WebEx, or Adobe Connect.

Face-to-face meetings can be difficult enough, but when people are meeting remotely, it presents unique challenges that must be addressed. Although we have discussed virtual meetings in other chapters, we will bring it all together here. Here are the steps to having great conference calls and virtual meetings.

CONFERENCE CALL OR
VIRTUAL MEETING?

By now you understand the power of visual flight recording to facilitate Holographic Thinking. Careful consideration of what you are trying to accomplish with the meeting can be the first determining factor in choosing a format. If you are brainstorming, matching and mismatching, or discussing a complex issue, you must have virtual flight recording on a shared screen that everyone can see. Even if the logistics of a person's location does not give that person access to a computer, anyone with a smartphone can use the virtual software's remote app to call in and see the screen. Obviously, if the person is driving or is somewhere with no Internet or cell service, this will not be possible. Such circumstances should be considered ahead of time in the preparation phase of the meeting.

However, if the agenda of your meeting concerns an update and understanding and interacting on that information, then an audio-only conference call is acceptable. For example, the executive committee of a board, consisting of the executive director, president, and vice president, has been meeting once a week by phone for 15 to 30 minutes to check in and discuss the day-to-day operations of the association. A group call has always worked well for that. However, when it was time to brainstorm fund-raising ideas with the whole board and decide which to pursue, that required the power of the shared visual screen.

When you are planning a remote meeting, step 1 is to ask, "What are we trying to accomplish?" Therefore, "What are the required logistics of the meeting participants?" Choose the appropriate format and inform all attendees accordingly.

ESTABLISH A "CALL IN BY" OR "LOG IN BY" TIME

In a phone or virtual meeting, it is essential to establish a "call in by" or "log in by" time. If you specify only a starting time for your call, you should expect some attendees to be late. With virtual meetings, maybe they can't find the e-mail with the log-in information or they are experiencing a computer glitch that requires a restart. If it's a conference call, people are likely to call in at the very last minute. And if something, such as an e-mail or a coworker, distracts the participants for just a minute or two, they will be late.

To ensure that people are present and ready to participate by the time you start the meeting, establish a call-in or log-in time about four to five minutes before the meeting starts.

Use Unusual Start and End Times

For example, "Log in between 8:53 and 8:57 a.m. The meeting will start promptly at 9:02 a.m." Weird times are memorable. They also force people to make calculations: "Let's see, at 8:45 I'll be on that side of the building. To get to my computer, it will take three minutes." The net result will be a greater likelihood of people calling in and logging in on time.

As the call organizer, be sure to stick to the unusual times for each agenda item (for example, "9:02 to 9:17 a.m., Questions on the new policy"). This will demonstrate that you are paying attention to and respecting time.

Start Exactly on Time Whether or Not the "Right" People Are There

I've said it many times before, but it is worth saying again. You must start on time, period! Otherwise, you train people to come late.

Even better, block latecomers from the call. You will have to do this only once or twice before everyone gets the message that you are serious about following the schedule you have established. It's true that some agenda items may suffer because the right people aren't there, but in the long run, participants will understand that you are serious, and they will make sure that they arrive on time for future calls.

If it is the type of meeting that requires a quorum to do business and you have to allow latecomers to join the meeting, start on time and do the agenda items that do not require a motion or a vote.

Allow Some Cacophony at the Beginning of the Meeting

Have everyone say hello simultaneously before you mute all participants (or ask everyone to mute themselves). This gives people a feeling of being in a virtual room together, which helps build rapport and unity among group members.

MAKE SURE EVERYONE KNOWS HOW AND WHEN TO MUTE THEMSELVES

It may seem obvious, but I know you have been in meetings in which you've heard dogs barking, pans clanging, water running, and so on. Make sure people know how, using the virtual meeting software, to mute themselves each time they finish speaking, and remind them to do so if they forget. When people call in, remind them to use the mute function on their phones whenever they finish speaking.

If someone forgets and you are using virtual meeting software, as the organizer, do not hesitate to mute them. If the meeting is by phone, this is one of those times when everyone is the copilot and should speak up to ask people to please mute themselves.

HAVE AN AGENDA

For a successful meeting, you need a Flight Plan, and that's the agenda. In a less formal phone-only meeting, a quick agenda can be created at the beginning of the call. For example, in the case of the three-person executive committee phone meeting, the first order of business is to hear from each person what items need to be gone over during the call and establish the order to do it.

In more formal and complex meetings, all participants should receive a copy of the agenda a few days before the meeting and have it in front of them. The agenda can also be projected on the shared screen, though once flight recording starts on a subject, that will cover up the agenda.

All the factors in Chapter 4, "The Art of the Agenda," apply. The agenda should be well thought out with realistic time frames so that the meeting ends on time without the need to cut items short.

ESTABLISH THE AIR TRAFFIC CONTROL CIRCULAR SPEAKING ORDER

A downside of conference calls is that you can't see people raise their hands when they have comments or questions. In virtual meetings it's too easy for people to either talk over each other or be too polite and say nothing. To ensure that everyone has a voice, include a speaking order on the agenda. In the more informal meeting, establish the circular order at the beginning of the call and stick to it. When appropriate, go around the virtual room and give every participant a chance to speak. When it's their turn, people can speak, pass, or say, "Come back to me."

If your conference call has a mix of some people who are face-to-face in a room participating via speaker phone while others are remote, let the remote individuals go first. It will help them feel more included.

AGREE ON NO MULTITASKING

The problem with conference calls and virtual meetings is that it's too easy for people to do other things while the meeting is going on. When attendees are multitasking, they think they are paying attention, but in reality, they are distracted. Agree ahead of time that people will not multitask. People multitask because they are trying to use time efficiently by doing two things at once. Let attendees know the meeting will be focused and will get done faster if they are not multitasking.

To create further accountability during the meeting, instead of a circular order, you can have a random order. In other words, the Air Traffic Controller will make sure everyone has a chance to speak, but in no particular order. When their turn comes up, they had better be ready. If the meeting is virtual, you may want to have webcams turned on. This will definitely create more accountability to stay focused. It also will create a big difference in how present and connected people will feel.

USE FLIGHT RECORDING

When dealing with complex issues, you want people to see the flight recording on a shared screen. But even in less formal phone conference meetings, you should still use flight recording, even though people may not be seeing the shared screen. Commitments by participants to follow up with action steps should be recorded, and complete notes should be sent to everyone after the call.

FLIGHT RECORDING WITHOUT A SHARED SCREEN

If, for whatever reason, a shared screen is not possible but seeing the visual totality is important, then after each person speaks, the Flight Recorder can read what he or she has written and receive confirmation from the speaker that it's accurate. For everyone to see the visual totality of the points made in a discussion, attendees also need to see it in front of them. Everyone else on the call should write the Flight Recorder's confirmed statement. In that way, everyone is creating the same visual totality, based on the discussion. It works in a pinch, but go for the shared screen whenever you can.

STANDARD FOLLOW-UP

After the call or virtual meeting, the Flight Recorder will e-mail the notes to all the participants. If the meeting is long and a number of different topics have been discussed, the Flight Recorder should break down the notes into separate e-mails with clearly labeled subject lines. This will increase follow-up after the meeting and help people find the notes again if needed.

UNMUTE EVERYONE AND HAVE SOME "GOOD-BYE" CACOPHONY

At the end of the meeting, have everyone unmute themselves and say good-bye to one another. Again, a little cacophony can give people the feeling that they have been together.

———

By utilizing these conference call and virtual meeting tips and having a well-thought-out agenda, you'll impress participants by ending on time. Once participants realize that a meeting won't drag on indefinitely, they will participate more enthusiastically . . . and come to future conference calls or virtual meetings better prepared and more engaged.

GREAT MOMENTS IN MEETINGS

The Good, the Bad, and the Boring

When I first joined my firm, we had a global video conference with close to a hundred participants in America, Europe, Australia, Scandinavia, Hong Kong, and Africa. One of the big partners in London was talking and was being very boring. This lad in Australia took his tie and pretended to hang himself. He probably just had London on his screen and didn't realize we were able to see him. People were laughing around the world. Though the big boss saw it too, he didn't do anything, but just carried on.

—*Head of Global Insight, Large global consulting firm*

SUMMARY

1. Conference call or virtual meeting?

   - Clarify what you are trying to accomplish.

     o *Have a virtual meeting with a shared screen:* If you are brainstorming, matching and mismatching, or discussing a complex issue, you must have flight recording.

    ○ *Have a conference call:* If the agenda of your meeting involves an update and understanding and interacting on information, an audio-only conference call is acceptable. However, a Flight Recorder should take notes and send them to everyone afterward.

2. Publish a call-in or log-in time four to five minutes before the start.

    • Pick unusual times—that is, log in between 8:53 and 8:57 a.m.

3. Start on time.

    • If you need a quorum, start with business that doesn't require a vote.

4. Allow some cacophony at the beginning of the meeting.

5. Make sure everyone knows how to mute themselves.

    • If someone forgets to do so and is making noise, be a copilot and speak up or ask the organizer to mute them.

6. Have an agenda that everyone has received and show it on-screen.

    • In a less formal phone conference, the first order of business is to create the agenda.

7. Establish a circular speaking order.

8. Agree on no multitasking.

    • Use random order to encourage accountability.

    • Turn on webcams to create accountability.

9. Use flight recording.

10. Follow up after the meeting.

11. At the end of the meeting, have everyone unmute themselves and say good-bye to one another.

13

TSA: How the Process Prevents the Problem Behaviors

An ounce of prevention is worth a pound of cure.

—Ben Franklin

emember our problem behaviors from Chapter 1? Now that you understand the Meeting Jet process, let's take a look at how it prevents those behaviors.

In the Cooperation Zone of behavior, there are four basic intents. People want to *Get it done*, *Get it right*, *Get along*, and *Get appreciated*.

People in a *Get it done* mode love the Meeting Jet process because the meeting starts and ends on time. Each agenda has a time frame that is also adhered to. Distractions are eliminated as the group stays task focused and on course. Agenda items are methodically processed complete with follow-up actions using the eight meeting processes. People do not repeat themselves because their contributions are recorded visually. Because the group arrives at Holographic Thinking, the discussions are complete, decisions are made instead of put off, things get done, and the meeting is always under control.

People in a *Get it right* mode also love the Meeting Jet process because the meetings start on time and end on time. Agenda items are processed in detail, extracting people's criteria through the matching and mismatching processes. Ideas are fully discussed, details and opinions are recorded, and those details are e-mailed to the individual participants for later use. Because of the completeness of the discussions and the flight recordings, people in a *Get it right* mode feel comfortable that the details are covered and the right decisions are being made.

People in a *Get along* mode love the Meeting Jet process because meetings start and end on time. There is no conflict. There is no dominance by overly assertive behaviors. Because we all focus on the same topic at the same time, using the same process, everyone is one big happy team. There is no conflict, no "rude," overly assertive behaviors. Since everyone's point of view counts, they feel compelled to share their opinions. They love it because everyone gets along.

People in the *Get appreciated* mode love the Meeting Jet process because meetings start and end on time. The Q eliminates the competition to speak, and so people give one another their full attention and they like attention. Since everyone's contribution is noted visually by the Flight Recorder, they can see that their point has been acknowledged, and they are likely to feel very appreciated. Though at first it may be hard for them to hold themselves back and wait their turn in the Q, the full attention and visual appreciation more than make up for it.

Note one important thing: everyone loves the process, no matter where they are in the Lens, when meetings start and end on time.

Since the Meeting Jet process addresses people's intent to *Get it done*, *Get it right*, *Get along*, and *Get appreciated*, there is no need for them to leave the Cooperation Zone. But let's examine further how the process neutralizes the risk of any Danger Zone behaviors.

TANKS

Tank behavior, which can take the form of an attack in which the Tank runs over you, originates out of a desire to *Get it done* and *Control*. Tanks will declare martial law when they feel things are out of control. But because the Meeting Jet process is so organized and efficient, there are no tangents, no stray comments, no repetitions, and no one who talks too much. Everyone is focused on the topic and decisive. Tanks feel like everything is under control. They also tend to be one of the best keepers of the process in the long term.

SNIPERS (MALICIOUS OR FRIENDLY)

Since you have to get in the Q to speak at a meeting, there is no room in the process for stray Sniper comments, whether they are malicious or just joking. Think about it. Will people get in the Q just to make some sarcastic comment? Unlikely, but if they did, it would probably happen only once because the Pilot would point out right away that the comment had nothing to do with the topic and the process. The orderliness of the process is not conducive to any form of sniping.

KNOW-IT-ALLS

The problem with Know-it-all behavior at meetings is that Know-it-alls go on and on to hear themselves speak, thereby shutting down other people. But because one's time in the Q is limited, this keeps the Know-it-all in check. Since people who are being Know-it-alls actually do know what they are talking about, the limited time to speak forces them to get to the point. The focus on topic and process facilitates their contribution. Know-it-alls also have some level of ego in play, so when the Flight Recorder captures their contributions visually for the group to see, their egos are satisfied.

THINK-THEY-KNOW-IT-ALLS

People exhibiting this behavior also like to hear themselves speak, but once again the time limit in the Q prevents them from doing that. Also, it is hard to put vague, unsubstantiated claims and generalizations on a flip chart. That will force Think-they-know-it-alls to contribute something of value or not speak. Otherwise, their behavior will be transparent to all, and they care about what people think of them. When they do have something to say and the Flight Recorder captures their contributions visually, their egos are likewise satisfied.

GRENADES

Since this behavior is the classic tantrum and originates out of a *Get appreciated* and *Attention-seeking* mode, Grenades are unlikely to blow because of the level of attention and appreciation people give one another during this process. Because there is no competition to speak, everyone genuinely pays attention to the person speaking.

People's contributions are visually recorded by the Flight Recorder for all to see, which makes them feel appreciated. Though Grenade explosions are often the result of multiple issues that have been building up, the Meeting Jet process prevents any such explosions from taking place at the meeting.

WHINERS AND NO PEOPLE

Whining and negativity begin in the *Get it right* and *Perfection* mode, but then they become generalized to create the sense that everything is wrong, nothing is right, and it will always be that way. However, because the meeting process is controlled, it makes it impossible for Whiners and No People to demoralize the group with negative generalizations.

If the group is brainstorming or matching and the Whiners or No People offer a negative, the Pilot can point out, "That is not what we are doing now." Once the group switches to mismatching, the Whiners and No People can revel in all their negative glory. But it doesn't make sense to write "Everything is wrong" on a flip chart, so it forces them to be specific. Specifics are the first step in problem solving. This turns the Whiners and No People into smoke detectors, pointing out to the group potential problems or negative criteria that need to be solved.

JUDGES

This behavior also begins in the *Get it right* and *Perfection* mode, but instead of being generalized like whining and negativity, it is overly focused on details that may not matter. However, through flight recording, the group arrives at Holographic Thinking and is able to take all factors into account. Through the rating process, the relative priorities of multiple factors are sorted. Time limits to speak prevent the Judges from taking the group off course with details that don't matter. Their eye for detail is harnessed and controlled so that their skills can be useful instead of annoying distractions.

YES, MAYBE, AND NOTHING PEOPLE

Their problem at a meeting is that they don't participate at all (the Nothing People) or they simply agree with everyone without expressing their true feelings (the Yes and Maybe People). But because there is no competition to speak and the more assertive behaviors are controlled, the Meeting Jet process makes it easy for them to contribute. In a circular order Q, Nothing People will contribute, even if it's only to say they agree with what has been said.

Also, because everyone is focusing on the same topic at the same time in the same way, it makes it safe for Yes, Maybe, and Nothing People to contribute. When the process turns to mismatching, everyone is looking at the cons of an idea together. They are not opposing anyone. People at the meeting are one big happy team that's getting along. This empowers Yes, Maybe, and Nothing People to come out and play and speak their true feelings.

The Danger Zone behaviors can quickly derail a meeting, and each one of them is nipped in the bud when you use the Meeting Jet process. Instead of a Danger Zone behavior triggering Danger Zone behaviors in others, people reinforce the positive Cooperation Zone behaviors, thereby leading to a productive, efficient, high-quality meeting.

For even more specific strategies to pull people out of the Danger Zone in other contexts or relationships, read *Dealing with People You Can't Stand*.

GREAT MOMENTS IN MEETINGS

The Whiteboard Snarky Wipeout

I had a director who would attend IT architecture working sessions even when his technical input was not needed but he had the authority to attend. He would make comments that were off the wall and distract the group. He would say one thing and then contradict himself five minutes later. He seemed to thrive on conflict and controversy. The end product of the meeting was a poor design.

One day I started taking notes on the whiteboard in front of the room on what people said. I innocently included whatever the IT director said. When he started seeing his stupid statements in print for the whole room to read, he stopped making provocative comments.

The practice has other benefits as well. We found mistakes were corrected before the meeting was over, disagreements were addressed during the meeting—not later—and consensus tended to stick because people could see all of the notes. Some people need to see, not just hear, to process information. After 15 years, I still use the practice at all levels.

—Project manager, Food manufacturing company

SUMMARY

1. The Meeting Jet process

   - Gives a feeling that the meeting is under control

2. Topic and process boxes to maintain focus

   - Eliminate sniping and irrelevant comments

   - Prevent tangents

- Make it safe for people with the intent to *Get along* because everyone is doing the same thing at the same time

3. Speaking order to balance participation

   - Prevents Know-it-alls from dominating the meeting

   - Makes it safe for more passive people to participate

4. Respect for time

   - People relax and are less likely to be in the Danger Zone because the meeting is on schedule and ends on time.

PART IV

IMPLEMENTING *the* MEETING JET PROCESS

14

Integrating the
Meeting Jet Process with
Robert's Rules of Order

Parliamentary law should be the servant,
not the master, of the assembly.
—GENERAL HENRY M. ROBERT

Many associations and boards I have worked with use *Robert's Rules of Order* to varying degrees as the standard guide to parliamentary procedure. They are the rules by which an organization runs business meetings to keep order. This is not so in companies. This chapter is about how to integrate the Meeting Jet process with *Robert's Rules*. If you do not use *Robert's Rules*, you can skip this chapter.

Once your group starts using the Meeting Jet process, many of *Robert's Rules* become unnecessary. However, many boards will still use *Robert's Rules* to conduct official votes and make decisions. Therefore, the Meeting Jet process needs to be integrated into *Robert's Rules*.

COMMON *ROBERT'S RULES*

Typically, the most frequently used *Robert's Rules* are as follows:

Motion: When a member of the board wishes the board to take action on an item, he or she must make a motion to that effect. For example, "I move that the board meeting be held in Hawaii on January 12." Technically, until such a motion is made, no discussion of the issue may occur, although many small boards do not strictly adhere to *Robert's Rules* in this area, particularly when an item of business has been placed on the agenda and requires some presentation of information before a decision is made.

Second the motion: Before a motion may be discussed, it must be seconded—that is, another member of the board must agree that the subject should be brought into the forum for discussion and a vote. Usually, the person seconding the motion is in favor of the motion, but in some cases, people may second a motion for the purpose of allowing discussion, and they may actually be opposed to the motion.

Call for the question: This is a request by a member that discussion cease and a vote on the issue at hand be taken. Frequently, this is a statement made without recognition from the chair, and it is simply a statement of that person's readiness to vote. If the chair recognizes the member, she or he may move that the question be called. If this is seconded, then a vote is taken on whether to stop debate on the current issue. A vote of two-thirds is required to stop debate. If the chair does not recognize the speaker, the chair uses his or her discretion as to when to put an issue to a vote. Recognition of a member is at the discretion of the chair.

Voting: Voting may be by voice ("All in favor, signify by saying 'Aye'"), by a show of hands, or by written ballot. On most issues, a simple majority is sufficient to pass an issue.

Summary of the Order by Which Things Are Done

1. Motion

2. Second

3. Discussion

4. Amendments to the motion (must be approved by both the motion maker and the seconder)

5. Call for question (optional)

6. Vote on the end of discussion if a motion to call the question has been made and seconded

7. Vote on any amendments

8. Vote on the motion

Since the Meeting Jet process is designed to foster high-quality discussions and analysis of ideas through brainstorming, matching, and mismatching, those processes cannot be allowed to be interrupted by *Robert's Rules*. For example, if during a discussion someone were to make a motion and have it seconded, then technically a discussion would need to ensue on that motion. This of course would suddenly change the topic and process as well as cut off any of those people who are still in the Q. This would be completely inappropriate to the Meeting Jet process.

MOTION TO ADOPT MEETING JET RULES

Once a group wants to try the Meeting Jet process, a motion needs to be made to try it and let it supersede *Robert's Rules*, except in relation to decision-making. The needed motion will be to adopt the Meeting Jet rules of order in relation to analyzing ideas via brainstorming, matching, mismatching, discussion, presentation, Q&A, and rating. After the necessary processes are complete, *Robert's Rules* for motions and voting to take action will apply.

Therefore, if someone in the speaking Q has a motion she wishes to make, when it is her turn, she can still state that she wishes to make a motion. The Air Traffic Controller will write an "M" next to her name, but the Q will continue. The complete discussion time will be allowed for the topic, as called for in the agenda.

Once the discussion is complete, the Pilot will come back to the person wishing to make the motion. The purpose of doing this is so that a motion cannot be used to cut people off from being heard. In my experience, a better alternative is to say that you don't make motions in the middle of a discussion. After the ideas are analyzed, and after matching, mismatching, and discussions are complete, and it's decision time, then it's time for motions. Calling for the question also would have to be eliminated because it can be used to cut people off from speaking and end discussions.

Robert's Rules are used because there usually are no speaking time limits or time frames for agenda items or clear processes other than discussion. Therefore, *Robert's Rules* are needed to move things forward. But the Meeting Jet process takes care of this much more effectively. Better to have clear time frames and clear processes and to complete high-quality discussions than to use *Robert's Rules* to ask for motions and amendments and then official votes.

When the Meeting Jet process is presented to a board that uses *Robert's Rules*, it will have to be motioned, seconded, and voted that the group try it and adjust the use of *Robert's Rules* appropriately. Once the group has decided that they want to continue to use the Meeting Jet process (which they will), a formal motion and vote needs to be taken to make that change. This change will then need to be written either in the organization's procedure manual or in the bylaws, if that's where using *Robert's Rules* is specified. For more details on using Meeting Jet with boards, see dealingwithmeetings .com.

GREAT MOMENTS IN MEETINGS

The Great Boss Centerpiece

Many years ago, I was a new manager at a new company, and one of the first few females to be hired in that position. I was giving my first big presentation and hoping to make a good impression. The conference room had a large table in the middle with plush chairs around it for the bigwigs, and there were less comfy chairs around the sides of the room. People kept pouring in.

Being new, I was naturally a bit nervous. As every last chair was filled, attempting to relax myself, I made a joke that the next person who walked in would have to sit on top of the table. While everyone was still laughing, who walked in next? Yes, our most senior executive director, R.G., who wanted to know what was so funny. I was just going to say, "Oh, nothing, let's get started now." But one of my colleagues repeated what I had said about sitting on the table, so R.G. promptly did exactly that. He climbed up onto the middle and sat with legs crossed, like a centerpiece, and stayed there through my entire presentation.

I tried not to get rattled. He was a very good sport about it, and he even complimented my presentation, but it was not the way I expected to make a first impression!

—R&D manager, Telecommunications company

SUMMARY

How the Meeting Jet Process Enhances *Robert's Rules*

1. By having a speaking order, everyone one is heard from.

2. By having time limits on all agenda items and turns to speak, calling for the question is unnecessary.

3. By flight recording, criteria are revealed and discussions are complete, which leads to clear and effective motions.

How to Implement the Meeting Jet Process with *Robert's Rules*

1. Make a motion to temporarily adopt the Meeting Jet process in relation to analyzing ideas and having discussions.

2. To formally adopt the process, make a motion, second it, and vote to do so in relation to analyzing ideas and having discussions.

3. Write down that decision in either the procedure manual or the bylaws if using *Robert's Rules* is specified there.

15

Cage Rattling 101: Bringing People on Board the Meeting Jet

Don't let the fear of striking out hold you back.
—BABE RUTH

Changing the habits of people in an organization and accepted corporate culture can seem a daunting task. Maybe you are not the one who organizes or runs the meetings but are simply the victim, ah, I mean an attendee at the meetings. The most important thing to keep in mind is that most people hate meetings. It wouldn't hurt to suggest to those who are in charge of meetings a process that will make meetings shorter, more focused, and more productive.

The overall steps to implementing the Meeting Jet process are as follows:

1. Start with the people responsible for running meetings and let them know there is a better way.

2. Create and present to them your Cage Rattling document of the potential dramatic benefits.

3. Give them a copy of this book so they understand the process and direct them to dealingwithmeetings.com for more information.

4. Suggest that the group try it twice as an experiment to see what happens.

5. Once the person in charge is on board, talk to participants to let them know there is a better way and utilize the resources at dealingwithmeetings.com to give them an understanding of the process.

THE CAGE RATTLING DOCUMENT

Let's examine a written strategy I affectionately call Cage Rattling. Cage Rattling is an effective way to bring people on board with new, even radical, ideas. It can be applied internally to create change within your organization.

The written word is powerful because it becomes physical; it is something you can see and remains the same over time. A verbal presentation is easily forgotten, even a compelling one. Even if you make an extremely persuasive verbal presentation, as soon as you leave, in floods a thousand other things asking for the person's attention, and where is your presentation? Gone. Now, this is not to discount the importance of the passion of a verbal presentation.

And if you make a verbal presentation, make sure you leave them with a document; it is more likely that they will follow through on it. An additional benefit is that they can show the document to others and bring them on board too. A passionate verbal presentation coupled with a document is very powerful.

THE THREE PARTS OF THE CAGE RATTLING DOCUMENT

In the first part, you want the reader's psychological agreement that what you're suggesting is undeniably important. In the second part, your goal is to shock them by proving that what they've just agreed is important is not happening or, even worse, is completely lost. You will prove that with facts and figures. In the third part, you offer a thoughtful solution that fulfills the intentions of the first part yet avoids the problems of the second part. Let's examine these in greater detail.

Part I: Begin with Intent

Just as every agenda item has a clear intent and purpose to orient people, the first line of the first paragraph begins with a question that includes the intent or is a statement of intent and then asks if the reader is interested in hearing more. Why a question? Because you want readers to have to mentally answer yes to it and open their minds to hearing more:

> Would you like to hear about a meeting process that keeps us focused and ensures that we hear from everyone?

or:

I read about a tried-and-true strategy that makes meetings shorter, more engaging, and more effective. It enables you to get things done more quickly at a higher quality. I'm wondering if we should try it as an experiment?

or:

Would you like to hear a strategy that prevents conflict and tangents at meetings?

Consider what specific issues your reader experiences at meetings, and rework the opener accordingly. Try tying it to company initiatives. If there are budget cuts happening and everyone is trying to do more with less, this might be compelling:

Would you like to hear about a strategy that makes our meetings shorter, yet more productive and, based on my research, can save us $50,000 a year?

How will you know it can save $50,000 a year? We'll get to that shortly. Stay tuned.

Mission statements can also be a source of inspiration. For example:

I know one of the pillars in our mission statement is this: "People and teamwork are our greatest assets." But it doesn't seem like the quality of our meetings reflects that. Would you like to hear about a meeting strategy that prevents conflicts, integrates different points of view, and fosters respect for what each team member brings to the table?

At this point, readers should be nodding. They are psychologically agreeing that what you are proposing is important, so your goal for Part I is almost accomplished. There is just one more thought to add. And it goes back to the other critical lens in every agenda item: "What do you want from them?" Tell the readers why you are presenting this idea to them. Is it because they are the only ones with the authority to move this forward? Or is it because you need advice on how to proceed? Always orient readers so that they know their role.

Part II: Use Some Shock Therapy

Part II contains factual examples that contradict what was just mentally agreed upon as important in Part I: "We say we value teamwork, but look at what we allow to happen in our meetings." Describe two to three examples. Be brief but clear. Include dates, facts, and numbers. Do not express emotions or even opinions— just stick to the facts.

One of the most important numbers to include is the cost. What is it costing the organization to allow this situation or policy to continue? Here are three ways you can arrive at these numbers.

Do Some Research

Get to all meetings on time for a few weeks and record the time wasted waiting for everyone to show up. Go to HR, let them know what you are doing, and ask if they can give you a per minute dollar number of what those people cost the company—a single total number. Be clear that you are sharing the calculation with only senior decision-makers to have them see the value of having a meeting process. In my research I talked to a number of HR directors. Most thought they could provide it, while some did not. If your HR does not want to provide this number for any reason, refer to an online database such as glassdoor.com, which can give you the average salary for different jobs in different geographic areas. With that, you can arrive at a reasonable estimate.

Then do some calculations. Take the average number of minutes wasted waiting that you tracked and multiply that by the dollars per minute that people cost. Multiply that by the estimated number of meetings per year in your department and—voilà!—you will have a shocking number.

Be creative, but be conservative. Whenever you are not sure and you need to estimate a number, assume it is lower than you think it is. That way, when people read it, if they know that it is more than what you are saying, they will be even more shocked.

Use Other People's Numbers

As mentioned in the Introduction, according to the Wharton Center for Applied Research, senior executives spend an average of 23 hours per week in meetings, and middle managers spend 11 hours. According to senior and middle managers, 44 percent of meetings are unproductive.[1]

A survey conducted by Harris Poll found that U.S. employees at large-sized companies (1,000 employees or more) consider that the number one obstacle getting in the way of work consisted of "wasteful meetings, not needed, not engaging, and inefficient."[2]

In the United States there are 36 to 56 million meetings held each day, and it is estimated that between $70 and $283 billion a year is spent on unproductive meetings.[3]

The value to organizations of improving their meetings is huge. If you have a management team with five people at an annual salary of $100,000 per person and they spend an average of 15 hours a week in meetings, your weekly direct meeting cost for only these five people is $4,076, and your annual cost is a shocking $212,000! If you can reduce that by 40 percent, you will save $85,000 per year!

Harvard Business Review found that 15 percent of an organization's total collective time is spent in meetings, and that percentage has increased every year since 2008.[4]

Tie these numbers to your company with an estimate.

Create a Hypothetical Example

Based on other people's numbers, you can create a hypothetical example. Consider your own schedule and that of your colleagues. How much time do you spend in meetings each week, and how many meetings do you have? Then do the math: time spent in meetings each week × the number of meetings each week × 52 weeks = total minutes. Then cite the Wharton study finding that 44 percent of meeting time is wasted. Take 44 percent of the total minutes you calculated, and that is the time you can save for more productive activities. That is "money" in the company's pocket.

You can do any or even all of these three: do some research, use other people's numbers, and create a hypothetical example.

I suggest you write three examples. Why three? It's the human generalization point. If we are driving and stop at three red lights in a row, we say, "All the lights are red today." If we run into three people in a bad mood, we say, "Everyone is in a bad mood today." It takes only three before people generalize. So if I were trying to persuade my manager to implement a meeting process, and I gave three examples of the issue and potential benefit, the psychological response in the reader would be, "Wow, this is a real issue, and the potential savings are huge!" Now you are speaking to an open mind. Time to propose the solution.

Part III: Solve the Problem

Your purpose in the third part of your document is to ensure that readers fully understand how your idea solves the problem. Handle any "yes, but" issues the reader might have by acknowledging those doubts, and then point out how your solution addresses them. If you don't yet know how to handle the doubt, just acknowledge its presence and indicate that you will figure out a way to solve it so the reader doesn't get stuck on this point. For example, "I realize we have to get everyone on board with this idea. I can survey them to see if they would like to do an experiment to improve our meetings."

Show value. What does the organization stand to gain by implementing your idea? Based on your calculations of the problem, you are ready to take this next step. In the last section, we calculated what people are worth and how much time and money is wasted waiting for people to show up. Or the total number of minutes spent in a year of meetings. Reiterate those numbers and add what time saved from meetings would do to increase productivity and improve morale.

Be conservative. What if you could shorten all meetings by only 20 percent? Now do the math. Show how that savings of time can be given back to everyone to do more productive things that support the company.

Last, specify the criteria for your solution. Why did you pick that specific solution to solve the overall problem? It won't cost anything? It's easy to implement for all types of meetings? You know the importance of criteria from Chapter 10. Show that your solution fulfills all relevant criteria in your specific situation.

As you know, when people have an objection or consideration, it's because they lock on to certain criteria. But in this Cage Rattling document, you have presented such a complete perspective that they probably will be more willing to tweak things to make it work.

There are no guarantees in life, but using this Cage Rattling document to communicate clearly will stack the deck in your favor.

YOUR NEXT STEP

Give them a copy of this book along with your Cage Rattling document so they understand the process. Get their agreement to try it as an experiment. Suggest that a copy of the book be purchased for each participant. Although this is good for my book sales, I do not suggest this to be self-serving. It is important for everyone to understand and, ultimately, own the process for themselves. It empowers them to use the process in other meetings.

Once the person in charge is on board, it's time to talk to your coworkers. Ask them how they feel about meetings and suggest to them there is a better way. You can use your Cage Rattling document with them too. Show them this book, or give them a copy, or point them to the resources at dealingwithmeetings.com.

PERFORM A TEST FLIGHT

Suggest that the group try the Meeting Jet process at two meetings to check it out. Most will be happy to try anything that might make their meetings shorter and more focused.

Once the group has agreed and the date is set, make the necessary preparations. First, make sure that the proper equipment will be available in the meeting location: the whiteboard for the Q and either the flip chart or a computer connected to a projector for the flight recording. Second, decide who is responsible for creating the agenda. Third, decide who will be the Pilot, the Air Traffic Controller, and the Flight Recorder. Along with the agenda, send a summary of the Meeting Jet process. You want people going into the meeting with an understanding of the process.

At the beginning of the first meeting, allow at least 10 minutes on the agenda to review the Meeting Jet process for everyone. Use the process to have the group decide what their auditory signal will be. Then run the meeting using the process.

At the end of the meeting, allow time for matching and then mismatching with regard to the meeting process. Flight record as usual. Use the circular order to make sure that everyone is heard from. In this case, when matching is the process, I would let people articulate as many matches as they have in each turn. The same is true for when the process switches to mismatching. Participants should be instructed to repeat matches that others have said if they agree with them (or mismatches when that's the specified process). Have the Flight Recorder put hash marks next to a match or mismatch each time it is mentioned. This will provide a clear vision of what works and what to focus on to improve the process. But don't make changes to the process yet that are based on this feedback. You need to try it at least one more time to give people a chance to get used to it.

You may also initiate the process in a more formal way by hiring one of our certified Meeting Jet trainers or me. In this case, we'll teach a group of facilitators within your organization the process so that they can teach it to others. I have found the best way to learn is simply to run real meetings using the process. Using internal facilitators, you will spread the process through the organization and reap huge savings in time and money while increasing quality and productivity.

GREAT MOMENTS IN MEETINGS

Llama Dung

We engineers are so good at solving problems that we sometimes forget to ask if a problem is posed correctly. Questioning the rationale behind things is useful. Consider the U.S. Army's llamas. In the early

1940s, so the story goes, the Army wanted a dependable supply of llama dung, as required by specifications for treating the leather used in airplane seats. Submarine attacks made shipping from South America unreliable, so the Army attempted to establish a herd of llamas in New Jersey. Only after the attempt failed did anyone question the specification.

Was llama dung really necessary, or could there be a local substitute? Subsequent research revealed that the U.S. Army had copied a British Army specification dating back to Great Britain's era of colonial expansion. The original specification applied to saddle leather. Great Britain's pressing need for cavalry in its many colonies meant bringing together raw recruits, untrained horses, and new saddles. The smell of new leather made the horses skittish and unmanageable. Treating the saddle leather with llama dung imparted an odor that calmed the horses. A century later they were treating the seats of military aircraft.

—Engineer, EDN Network[5]

SUMMARY

1. The overall steps to implementing Meeting Jet are as follows:

   - Start with the people responsible for running meetings and let them know there is a better way.

   - Create and present to them your Cage Rattling document that describes the potential dramatic benefits.

   - Give them a copy of this book so that they understand the process and direct them to dealingwithmeetings .com for more information.

- Suggest that the group try it twice as an experiment to see what happens.

- Once the person in charge is on board, talk to coworkers to let them know there is a better way, and utilize the resources at dealingwithmeetings.com to give them an understanding of the process.

2. Create a Cage Rattling document.

- Part I: Begin with Intent

  o Consider the specific issues the reader experiences.

  o Phrase the intent as a question or finish with a question.

- Part II: Use Shock Therapy

  o Provide factual examples that contradict what the person mentally agreed was important in Part I.

  o Count the cost.

    » Do the research.

    » Use other people's numbers.

    » Create a hypothetical estimate.

- Part III: Solve the Problem

  o Handle or acknowledge "yes, but" issues.

  o Show value to the organization with numbers.

  o Specify your criteria for the solution.

16

Finale and Next Step: How We Came to Meet

You miss 100 percent of the shots you don't take.

—Wayne Gretzky

As we begin the descent to our destination, which is you equipped with the strategies to transform your meetings, I'd like to share a brief history of how this book came to be in your hands.

My father was a German thrown into the ghetto in Lodz, Poland, where he met and married my mother, who was from Lodz and an identical twin. In August 1944, they were sent to Auschwitz. Identical twins usually were turned over to Dr. Mengele for experiments. They were selected once, but they managed to get out of it. My father was selected for the gas chambers three times, but his ability to speak perfect German and his electrical skills enabled him to survive.

In January 1945, the Red Army was advancing quickly. The German military and German civilians were fleeing west toward the Allied forces. Auschwitz was liquidated, and my mother and her sisters were among 1,000 girls they took on a death march through the snow. They were the tail end of the German retreat. On a so-called rest break, they were ordered to dig ditches in the frozen road to slow down the Russian tanks.

It was January, bitter cold. They were hardly dressed and were starving. They had no food and would eat frozen grass. They were weak, the ground was frozen, and it was very difficult to dig.

One night, as they stopped to camp, my mother broke down and began to cry. A German officer called her over and demanded to know what she was crying about. My mother said, "I can't stand it anymore. I'm freezing, starving. Just kill me. I want this to be over." He said, "Look at me." She looked into his blue eyes—blue eyes she would see in her mind for the rest of her life. He was wearing glasses without frames. He was older than the average German soldier, maybe in his late forties. He said, "This is not the time to die. The war is almost over. It is us who will die and you who will live. You can make it, just watch yourself." He then tore his sandwich in half and handed it to her. Then he ordered her to stand guard in front of one of the fires at the camp.

The next day my mother had renewed hope. She looked for an opportunity and noticed two things: when she marched through deserted German towns and the road curved in a crescent, there was a point where the guards couldn't see her. That night, when they stopped to camp, she noticed that there were many minutes at a time when there were no guards to be seen. There were only 70 guards and about 1,000 girls. At one of those moments, she just got up and walked away.

She entered an evacuated German village. Looking for a place to hide, she found a house and scratched the frost off the window to peek inside. There was a Christmas tree with ornaments, but even better, there was fruit hanging from it: apples. She broke into the house and devoured an apple, but before she could feel the joy of freedom, she realized that she had left her two sisters back at the camp. She was certain they would think she was dead, which could be "the straw that breaks the camel's back" for them. She also knew they couldn't make it much longer either. But what should she do? She had already escaped! It was only a few seconds before she thought, "I cannot live the rest of my life knowing that maybe I could've done something. If I can do this once, I can do this twice. I'll sneak back, and we'll get away together."

So she hid some fruit on her person and snuck back to where her sisters and friend were. She explained the two opportunities. They made a pact that they would do it.

On the march the next day, when the road curved just right and the guards couldn't see, they made a break for it. My mother found a barrel and hid for hours. It was nightfall when she came out. The first thing she noticed was silence, and that's when she realized, "I'm free. Just like that. All things pass." One by one they all appeared, and after a jubilant reunion, they went into a nearby house.

It was decorated for Christmas. The table was set for four, with fine Rosenthal china for the holidays, as if they were expected. They found food prepared in the kitchen. That's how quickly German civilians evacuated in fear of the advancing Red Army. They sat down to a meal the likes of which they never thought they would eat again. When they were done, my mother looked at the fine hand-painted Rosenthal china and said, "We didn't live to wash dishes." They wrapped everything up in the tablecloth and threw it out the window.

My mother eventually made her way back to Lodz, and she got a job with an organization that registered returning refugees, connecting them with their families if alive or helping them find a place to live.

One day a refugee came in, still wearing a concentration camp uniform. He recognized her, although my mother didn't recognize him. It turned out that he was their next-door neighbor and a close friend of my mother's older sister, who was 20 years older than she. He broke down and started to cry, "The war has taken everything from me. You didn't even recognize me. My daughters are dead, my wife is dead, I wish I were dead. Why did I have to live?"

My mother said, "They're not dead. They came in last week. I can take you to them."

The man fell on his knees, grabbed her hand and started kissing it, and said, "What can I do for you? How can I repay you?"

My mother, just to get her hand back, offhandedly said, "Maybe someday you can bring my husband to me."

My father, in contrast, had been transferred from Auschwitz to concentration camps in Austria, and he wasn't liberated until the day after the war ended, five months later than my mother. He was traveling back to Poland with another refugee, who had family in Lodz. The other refugee's family owned a pharmacy there, so when they arrived, that was the first place they went. When new refugees came to town, people crowded around, asking them who they were and whom they were looking for. My father named the person he was looking for. A man stepped forward and said, "I know Simone. I can take you to her." And it was that man who brought my mother her husband.

And so a single decision of a German soldier in 1945 has come down through time to meet you in this moment now. All the miracles of my parents' survival (and there were many more) and the multitude of miracles in your life, both known and unknown, have brought us together, to this book being in your hands.

It is my hope that the strategies in this book will empower you to make a positive difference in the world by making every group you associate with more successful and effective. You can do it! You are now an agent of change who has the ability to turn conflict and polarization into communication and cooperation.

> *Never doubt that a small group of thoughtful,*
> *committed citizens can change the world;*
> *indeed, it's the only thing that ever has.*
> —MARGARET MEAD

Additional Resources

For resources related to this book, please visit www.dealingwith meetings.com.

For other books, audios, videos, training kits, and more, visit:

www.rickbrinkman.com

YouTube: Dr. Rick Brinkman

Facebook: Conscious Communication

SPEAKING AND TRAINING

Dr. Rick regularly delivers keynotes and custom internal training to fulfill your learning objectives. To check availability or discuss what Dr. Rick might do for you, please e-mail:

seminars@rickbrinkman.com

THE ONLINE COURSE: CONSCIOUS COMMUNICATION UNIVERSITY

Seven hours of entertaining video and interactive training (Figure A.1) that follow the content of the book *Dealing with People You Can't Stand*. SCORM Compliant for LMS.

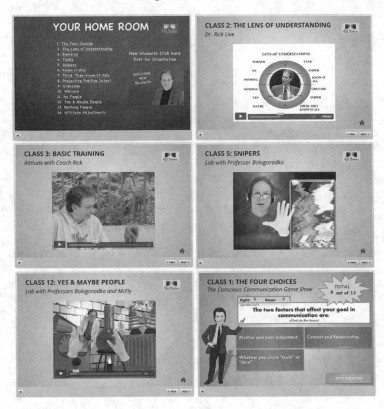

FIGURE A.1 Homeroom, Dr. Rick Live, Coach Rick, the Lab, and Game Show Modules for Each Class

If you have a question or want to discuss licensing internal trainers, or if you are interested in becoming a licensed trainer, or if you would like to share a communication or meeting success story, I'd love to hear from you! Please feel free to write me at:

dr.rick@rickbrinkman.com

Notes

Introduction

1. Cited in Daniel Goleman's article "Recent Studies Help Explain Why Some Meetings Fail," *New York Times* Science Section, June 7, 1988. This study was done by Dr. Lynn Oppenheim, a psychologist for the Wharton Center for Applied Research.
2. Michael Mankins, "The Ripple Effect," *Harvard Business Review*, April 8, 2014.
3. Harris Poll on behalf of CareerBuilder from February 11 to March 6, 2015.
4. Elise Keith, "55 Million: A Fresh Look at the Number, Effectiveness, and Cost of Meetings in the U.S.," Lucid Meetings blog, December 4, 2015, http://blog.lucidmeetings.com/blog/fresh-look-number-effectiveness-cost-meetings-in-us.

Chapter 15

1. Cited in Daniel Goleman's article "Recent Studies Help Explain Why Some Meetings Fail," *New York Times* Science Section, June 7, 1988. Study done by Dr. Lynn Oppenheim, a psychologist for the Wharton Center for Applied Research.
2. Harris Poll on behalf of CareerBuilder from February 11 to March 6, 2015.
3. Elise Keith, "55 Million: A Fresh Look at the Number, Effectiveness, and Cost of Meetings in the U.S.," Lucid Meetings blog, December 4, 2015, http://blog.lucidmeetings.com/blog/fresh-look-number-effectiveness-cost-meetings-in-us.
4. Michael Mankins, "The Ripple Effect," *Harvard Business Review*, April 8, 2014.
5. Richard Quinnell, "Beware: Llama Dung," EDN Network, May 19, 2015.

Index

About the Author

 **Dr. Rick Brinkman** is a top keynote speaker and trainer on the subject of Conscious Communication for leadership, teamwork, customer service, and effective meetings. He began his public practice in 1987 and has shared his expertise with millions of people via keynotes and trainings, radio, television, print interviews, and numerous bestselling books, videos, and audio programs. He has performed over 4,000 programs in 17 countries to share his human behavior insights and practical communication strategies. He is known for his unique presentation style of educating through entertainment, using stand-up comedy and storytelling to help people remember and act on the communication skills he teaches.

His clients have included the Astronaut Corps at NASA, the office of the undersecretary of defense, the FBI, Lucasfilm, Sony Pictures, Boeing, Lockheed Martin, Texas Instruments, Merck, Adobe, and a multitude of other organizations and professional associations.

He has been featured as a communication expert in print, radio, and television media, including the *Wall Street Journal*, the *New York Times*, *USA TODAY*, *O Magazine*, CNN, and CNBC.

He is the coauthor of the international bestseller *Dealing with People You Can't Stand*, which is in its third edition and has been translated into 25 languages. He is also the coauthor of four other books: *Dealing with Difficult People*, *Dealing with Relatives*, *Life by Design*, and *Love Thy Customer*.

For more information, please visit:

www.dealingwithmeetings.com

www.rickbrinkman.com

To contact Dr. Rick Brinkman, e-mail him at dr.rick@rickbrinkman.com.